To

Upright Bass
The Musical Life and
Legacy of Jamil Nasser

Keeper
of
the
Upright
Legacy
Peace

Upright Bass
The Musical Life and
Legacy of Jamil Nasser

A Jazz Memoir

MUNEER NASSER
Foreword by Ron Carter
Vertical Visions Media Group
Gaithersburg
2017

FIRST EDITION
Cover design by Aaron Hernandez and Muneer Nasser
Library of Congress Control Number: 2017909441
ISBN-13: 9780692895986
ISBN-10: 0692895981

CONTENTS

FOREWORD

You may call him George Joyner, the bassist who arrived on the 1956 New York jazz scene with the great pianist Phineas Newborn and took it by storm. Then he garnered wider exposure on the LP *All Mornin' Long* with Red Garland, John Coltrane, Donald Byrd, and Arthur Taylor. The title track, a hard drivin' blues, filled one side of this album. George's prominent bass notes resonated with such power and sincerity, he developed a reputation as a must-hear bassist. Consequently, I purchased any recording on which he played bass.

You may call him Jamil Sulieman, the man who possessed a profound, yet practical view of the world—especially the jazz scene—its politics, its culture, its vitality, its historical importance, and certainly its music.

You may call him Jamil Nasser, longtime partner in the Ahmad Jamal Trio, whose bass lines contributed to its well-tuned engine like precision.

Off the bandstand, as the vice president of the Jazz Foundation of America, he arranged the free medical care and financial assistance that continues to insure the survival of jazz artists.

Moreover, Jamil's entrepreneurial spirit and business acumen birthed his Kings Series, which presented special concerts like the first annual Beale Street Music Festival.

If you called him using one of these names, he would turn, greet you with a great, big smile, and a serious handshake.

As for me, I called him . . . my friend.

Ron Carter

PREFACE

The huge clarion sound of Richard "Notes" William's trumpet blared down Bleecker Street as Dad, my brother Umar, and I walked towards the Village Gate. Max Roach was leaving as we arrived; Dad introduced us and mentioned that Umar plays the drums. Max said, "Bring your son over, so I can check him out." Just before taking us backstage, he said, "Watch everyone, if you have any questions, ask." I recall us being the only kids in the club. Bassist Sam Jones said, "Jamil, where did you get those boys from . . . they're not yours." They laughed and talked briefly. Then Dad pointed to a man playing a baby bass, "Get his autograph," he signed, Philly Joe Jones. A few feet from Mr. Jones stood Woody Shaw cleaning his trumpet. "My son would like an autograph," Dad said. Woody put the horn down and signed my paper—without saying a word. Sensing my perplexity, Dad said, "Woody can be temperamental at times," as we walked away. The musicians exchanged firm handshakes and bear hugs as they gathered to honor the legacy of the late, great trumpeter Blue Mitchell. In June 1979, "Blue in the Night" featured Woody's Quintet, downstairs, and the Heath Brothers, upstairs, so we moved between two bandstands. Melba Liston, Milt Hinton, Cedar Walton, Jon Faddis, and Milt Jackson were among the musicians in the audience. They set the Gate on fire and the blaze intensified when Virgil Jones, Jon Faddis, Danny Moore, Jimmy Owens, Richard Williams, and

Tommy Turrentine ended the memorial with a supreme trumpet fanfare on "Summertime."

The Village Vanguard, Saint Peter's Church, Sweet Basil, and Condon's were among the many other venues we frequented. On some nights, Dad played. On others, we went to listen. Besides clubs and concert halls, Dad often took us to Montauk Point, Sag Harbor, and other Long Island fishing haunts that required hours of travel time. As the resident historian, I asked many questions on these trips. And his answers, conveyed in the African griot tradition, with vocal impressions and gestures, revealed a litany of stories about music, spirituality, politics, and life.

Ninety-five of the 100-bestselling jazz biographies on Amazon focus on bandleaders, not the sidemen. I use the term sidemen with ambivalence, because the bass is not a side instrument, but the very foundation of a jazz ensemble. The walking bass line establishes the pulse and outlines a composition's harmonic structure. Bill Johnson, George "Pops" Foster, Jimmy Blanton, Wellman Braud, Oscar Pettiford, Walter Page, and Ray Brown were great bassists who expanded its role beyond timekeeping and harmonic support to functioning as a melodic and solo instrument. In addition, Page, John Kirby, Red Callender, Pettiford, Charles Mingus, Ron Carter, and my father fulfilled dual roles as support bassists and bandleaders.

My father developed a warm, sonorous tone, a deep melodic sense, impeccable time, and big ears. The great pianist Monty Alexander said, "Jamil's well-crafted solos made me laugh and shake my head in wonder." I have seen jazz listeners erupt in laughter as Dad quoted, "Hail to the Chief" or "Down by the Riverside." Moreover, his discography includes over one-hundred commercially released and self-produced recordings with great musicians such as John Coltrane, Gene Ammons, Lou Donaldson, Al Haig, George Coleman, Randy Weston, and Ahmad Jamal. Yet jazz books and magazines often overlook his legacy.

For example, a recent publication, *The History of Jazz* (2011), made the following statement about Ahmad Jamal's career:

"Drummer Vernel Fournier and bassist Israel Crosby were unsurpassed at swinging while retaining the most subdued dynamic level. Together they formed one of the most underappreciated rhythm sections of the 1950s. Jamal's later work found him in a variety of settings, sometimes experimenting with electronics or performing with string accompaniment. The quality of these efforts is mixed, but the best of them—typically find him at the acoustic piano in a small-combo setting—are on par with his milestone recordings from the 1950s."[1]

The Awakening, a milestone 1970 recording, demonstrates the powerful, empathetic support of Jamil Nasser and Frank Gant, which thrilled audiences for over a decade; however, the author failed to mention their names.

Nevertheless, my father's hard-swinging, bluesy, and melodic style fueled his rise through the competitive ranks of his peers: Paul Chambers, Wilbur Ware, Doug Watkins, and Sam Jones.

Furthermore, he realized the jazz industry, which he challenged and attempted to reform, would never acknowledge his contributions. At a memorial, he organized for the late, great, tenor saxophonist Harold Vick, he said, "We in the trenches of the jazz business are tired of seeing our kings leave this earth without proper recognition." For this reason, he collected newspaper and magazine articles, recordings, interviews, concert flyers, and photos to self-document his musical journey and activism.

Dad asked me to write a memoir instead of an autobiography. When I conducted our first interview on January 31, 2003, I felt his sense of urgency, his sense of now or never, and the pauses in his speech confirmed this feeling. Although, he was lucid in this period, the next year, he received disturbing news—Alzheimer's disease. The diagnosis imposed time constraints because it eventually undermined his ability to communicate.

Dad and I made a beeline out of the door to interview the late, great drummer Earl "Buster" Smith who recalled vividly their experiences in North Africa, Europe, and Russia. Buster expired just several months after our last interview.

Over a span of fourteen years, I interviewed over fifty musicians, family, and friends. The internet and libraries in New York City, San Diego, Memphis, and Washington DC provided much-needed historical context. Lastly, I spent many hours sifting through my father's personal archive and excavating thirty years of personal conversations on music.

My father's field of activity transcended playing great bass lines and solos. As an educator, jazz advocate, herbalist, record producer, concert organizer, fiction writer (*Big Willie*), actor, and spiritual counselor, he rendered service to fellow musicians, students, and people in general.

Upright Bass documents his experiences as an African American, Muslim jazz musician. Unfortunately, the greatest information repositories are not libraries, archives, or universities, but the cemeteries that contain both the remains and untold stories of many great artists. My father didn't want to relegate his history or that of his fellow musicians to conjecture. Consequently, Upright Bass contains the valuable insights of those musicians. I had the challenging task of weaving interview transcripts, reviews, liner notes, meeting agendas, and notes into the historical narrative that follows.

ACKNOWLEDGMENTS

I would like to first thank Allah for unwavering support and guidance. My family (Leah, Amir, Layilah, and Sakeenah) has sacrificed and stood by me through it all. I would like to extend a heartfelt thanks to Umar Nasser, Zaid Nasser, Aliyah Nasser, Karimah Nasser, Baano Nasser, Najee Nasser, Jamillah Nasser, Kareem Nasser, Idris Nasser, Debra Alyssa Nasser, Yasmin, Asiya, Sumayyah, Maryum, Ahmed, Aisha, Fatimah, Ameenah, Jamil, Karimah, Asma, Muhammed, Yousef, and Nura Nasser. Dorothy Robinson, Phillip Andre Joyner, Clyde Ester Crawford, Norman Simmons, Jimmy Owens, John Handy, George Coleman Sr., George Coleman Jr., Lou Donaldson, Randy Weston, Monty Alexander, Irvin Salky, Calvin Newborn, B.B. King, Harold Mabern Jr., Frank Gant, Phil Schaap, Buster and Marvin Smith, Paul Jeffrey, Robin D.G. Kelly, Ned Otter, Adam Brenner, Marvin Goffe, Chris Bodiford, Andrea Payne, Fred Foss, Rusty Hassan, Joe and Sandra Selman, Atiba Taylor, Big Black, Verner and Maureen Webb, Tiacoh Sadia, Wanda Bamberg Tia, Brenda Siler, E. Ethelbert Miller, Karen Francis, Willie Thomas, Charlie Morrison, Lillian Terry, Tina France, James Holt, Malaika Adero, John Hope Franklin Jr., Tim Smith, Floyd Newman, Julian Euell, Ray Mosca, Toni Blackman, Johnny Garry, Valerie Cross, Aisha, Nurideen, and Ibrahim Tyner, Barry Harris, Larry Ridley, Jamila Sulieman,

Angela Shoffstall, Charlie Joyner, Joseph Jones, Tina France, Jimmy Heath, Adam Markowicz, Leroy Williams, Whitmore John, Askia Muhammad, Polly Walker, Ron Carter, Howard and Patsy McCree, Michael and Kenny Welch, Jimmy Wormworth, James King, Allyn Johnson, John R. Lamkin III, Cobi Narita, Paul Ash, Frank Smith, Judith Corey, Rachel Elwell, Reginald Cynthe, Juan and Rico Gray, Brother Tehuti Evans, Junious Levi Whitaker, Shakir Bakari Williams, Willard and Suzan Jenkins, Michael Thomas, Patrice Joyner, Montgomery County Arts Council, Harold King, Tony Addison, Russell T. West, Michael Subhan Spencer (photographic assistance), Ellen Carter, Antonio Parker, and my beloved cat, Fred.

OVERTURE

Why must I be a junkie to record with John Coltrane, Red Garland, and Gene Ammons? I thought my eighteen-hour practice sessions were the key.

In 1956, I encountered this vexing dilemma as a young musician coming from Memphis to New York City. My curious mind led me to question and answer sessions with elder musicians like Lester Young and Papa Jo Jones. In fact, Papa Jo's mentorship steered me around the minefield of loose women, drugs, exploitative club owners, and greedy record executives. I buried far too many young musicians who came to New York clean-cut, full of ambition, only to perish with needles in their arms. I survived because of the merciful Creator, the good values instilled by my parents, and a healthy dose of common sense. Born in Memphis during the Depression Era, I watched my parents struggle with courage and determination to maintain a growing family. My father taught us about our proud ancestors who mastered agriculture and possessed an entrepreneurial spirit that commanded respect.

Speaking of music and business, the late, great trumpeter-composer W.C. Handy worked in New Orleans and many other places but dropped anchor in Memphis. Beale Street, the Mid-South cultural epicenter, produced great blues, jazz, gospel, and country musicians who stimulated his creative imagination. The legacies, however, of jazz musicians like "Lil" Hardin Armstrong, Jimmie

Lunceford, Buster Bailey, Phineas Newborn Jr., Calvin Newborn, George Coleman, Booker Little, Louis Smith, Evans Bradshaw, Harold Mabern, Frank Strozier, Sonny Criss, me, and many others are unheralded. For example, designating Memphis as "The Home of the Blues," obliterated our legacy as jazz artists with the stroke of a pen: we must write our history.

George Leon Joyner is my birth name; however, I chose the name Jamil Sulieman Nasser after converting to Islam. Jamil means beautiful. Sulieman is the Arabic equivalent of Solomon, and Nasser means helper. One night, I called the radio station, WKCR New York, to settle a dispute between two callers concerning how Jamil Nasser and Jamil Sulieman were two different people. They didn't realize I recorded and performed under three different names.

As an African American Muslim jazz musician, I experienced two levels of discrimination: color and religion. My conversion to Islam, for reasons I'll explain later, cut my work volume in half. Nevertheless, Islam gave me the discipline to eschew self-destructive vices, and the confidence to challenge injustice inside and outside the music industry.

Playing with Willie Mitchell, B.B. King, Phineas Newborn, Oscar Dennard, Randy Weston, Ahmad Jamal, George Coleman, Al Haig, and Lou Donaldson fulfilled my highest musical aspirations. I performed for kings, queens, world leaders, and common people on five continents and faced life-threatening situations like false imprisonment in South America and CIA sponsored harassment in North Africa.

When historian, Phil Schaap, interviewed me on his "Lost Master's Series," I promised to textualize a more detailed analysis of Oscar Dennard's history. Dennard's pianistic genius propelled our group, the New York Jazz Quartet, to and through great concerts in Europe, Russia, North Africa, and Poland. As independent cultural emissaries, we played behind the Iron Curtain two years before Benny Goodman's state department tour. Dennard's legacy has eluded the pages of jazz history; unfortunately, he was murdered in Cairo—a victim of international politics. With a heavy heart, I revisit this history.

Although, playing music is rewarding from an artistic standpoint, the music business resembled a plantation consisting of house and field musicians. I wanted more money and decided to pursue financial freedom in the real estate market. Moreover, selling houses enabled me to come off the road and meet my obligations as a father.

After many years of functioning in a supportive role, I felt compelled to expand my leadership and organizational skills. For instance, I produced the first annual Beale Street Music Festival and a two-day festival dedicated to Red Garland that featured George Coleman, Lou Donaldson, Bill Hardman, Phineas Newborn, and Clifford Jordan.

In the many books, magazines, and newspapers I have read over the last fifty years, I noticed how writers twist jazz history to exalt the student and bury the master. In print and broadcast media, I rectified their inaccuracies and made suggestions for improving the status of jazz artists. The old spiritual, "Nobody Knows the Trouble I've Seen," suggests the deafening silence that befalls artists who pass away with untold stories. Consequently, our history becomes a mystery thereby subjecting our children to the risk of repeating our mistakes and disregarding our contributions. My life has included great musical moments alongside the love and support of family, friends, and fans. Upright Bass chronicles my journey as an African American, Muslim jazz musician in life, music, and business.

1

First Notes

Jamil told me a wonderful story about his first performance. Three weeks after he picked up the bass, he got his first gig. I asked, 'Well, did you know the music?' He said, 'No,' I just made sounds and the sounds worked!

—Jimmy Owens

The talent shows at Booker T. Washington High School were like Hollywood coming to Memphis for us kids. Many of our dreams of stardom were born right there on that stage.

—Maurice White

One of my early inspirations passed on before I was born, my great-grandfather, Peter Sweeten. Dad told us, "Grandpa Peter, despite being born a slave (1845) in Coldwater, Mississippi, possessed an insatiable desire for freedom. So, he purchased both his freedom and two-hundred acres of land in Tate County. Furthermore, Grandpa Peter provided the plows, the seeds, and the farm tools for his sharecroppers, who received one-third of the corn, one-third of the cotton, and some took half of the crops produced.

As a landowner, he earned more money and attempted to persuade local Coldwater farmers to purchase land, but they couldn't see his vision, and the meetings degenerated into shouting matches. Thus, he concluded, Negroes would never achieve economic independence or the power it could create. Grandpa Peter often came home with cuts and bruises from fighting disrespectful white people and Negroes. His last wife not only poisoned him but also sold his valuable timber and retained possession over his acreage. In 1923, he expired with fifteen-hundred dollars in the bank and no will. Dad and his siblings had to sue their stepmother to receive some portion of the estate.

Born in January 1871, my paternal grandfather, Andrew "Cap" Joyner, produced crops and rented land to local farmers. He used to take me along when he ran errands, and I can remember white and black farmers consulting him concerning the optimal planting times for fruits and vegetables. I heard him tell a farmer, "You're supposed to plant vegetables that grow underground like turnips and potatoes on the dark side of the moon and over ground crops like corn during the full moon. If you don't plant your corn tomorrow morning, come harvest time, you will have dry stubs on your stalks." Storeowners on Front Street wouldn't purchase cottonseeds without his approval.

My father, James Henry Joyner Sr., was born in Coldwater, Mississippi to Andrew and Betty Joyner on July 30, 1899. And Claude Vivian Joyner, my mother, was born in Franklinton, Louisiana to John and Marianna Wricks on June 20, 1907. They married in Memphis on October 20, 1927 and remained so just a few months' shy of seventy-years.

I was born on June 21, 1932 in Memphis, Tennessee, the fourth of eleven children. My brothers and sisters include Marjie, James Jr., Dorothy, Helen, Phillip, Williametta, Lois, Clyde Ester, Charles, and Troy. The older siblings were born during the Depression Era, and Memphis wasn't immune to its effects. I often marveled over how my parents fed and sustained us during this bleak period. We lived on 966A Porter Street in South Memphis. My parents were great people who instilled the core values of respect for the Creator, integrity, and honesty . . . if we stepped out of line, an ass-whuppin' followed. For example, my sister Dorothy and I went across the street to the Bethlehem Community Center and stayed beyond our curfew. Mama met us on the porch with a braided switch and wore us out. One time, she caught me smoking a cigarette and made me smoke a huge cigar. Although I feigned disgust, it was the best cigar I ever smoked.

My mother, an excellent vocalist and pianist, led the family choir singing hymns at home. And Dad was a master chef who often worked double shifts because country clubs and restaurants throughout Memphis valued his culinary skills. Together, they raised a close-knit family with an impeccable reputation throughout Memphis. We worshipped at Mt. Nebo Missionary Baptist Church every Sunday. And the soulful gospel music I heard struck a sensitive chord. The spirit hit me at a Wednesday night prayer meeting, and I prayed for twenty minutes, "Mama and Daddy been fighting over money, but I know you can work it out Lord . . ." I exposed some of our private domestic issues—much to their embarrassment.

As a child, I played football, baseball, and ran track. The thrill of competition and the physical fitness demands captivated me. Then Dad took me to see, Satchel Paige, the legendary pitcher for the Kansas City Monarchs. Paige called in the outfielders and struck out every batter. We cheered like crazy for him. His confidence and poise inspired me to pursue athletics professionally. So, I started training as a boxer and developed enough skill to win the Bantamweight Championship at fifteen years old. After the fight, however, I looked in the mirror at the cuts and bruises on my face and couldn't believe I won . . . boxing as a career option ended with this match.

A few days later, I heard "Near You" on the radio and tran-scribed the melody by ear: *"Near You" was written by a Nashville bandleader named Francis Craig, and his recording of the tune had a repeating left-hand piano line that could indeed bring to mind a throb-bing drill. The independent Bullet label had released it as the B-side of a number called "Red Rose." But it was "Near You" that got picked up on radio stations throughout the South, spread to the rest of the country, and ultimately reached number one on the Billboard charts (1947). It stayed there for seventeen weeks."*[2]

Mama found a piano teacher who came by the house every week. I played more by ear than by sight-reading, so I asked him to play my next lesson and memorized it. During my recital, I was supposed to play two prepared pieces and sight-read one. I played the first two selections well, then composed a song in lieu of sight-reading ending with some fancy passages I'd worked out and the people cheered. Breaking the silence that followed, my teacher said, "I enjoyed that too, but he didn't read one note on the music paper."

The following week, my piano teacher asked Mama, if he could take me to a movie called *The Beast with Five Fingers*. He bought popcorn, we took our seats, the lights dimmed, and he reached for my zipper. I smacked his hand and said, "If you ever come back, I will tell my parents everything." Mama kept asking, "I wonder what happen to him?"

In 1945, I entered my first year at Booker T. Washington High School: *"Booker T. Washington High School was the first high school for African Americans in Memphis. Exactly when 'We lead and others follow' became Booker T. Washington's motto is uncertain. It is certain, however, that it inspired a desire for high achievements among its students."*[3]

Professor W.T. McDaniel led the band at Booker T. Washington. "McDaniel had an open mind and encouraged his students—who affec-tionately called him "Mr. Mac"—to explore newer music forms of the day such as bebop. Calvin Newborn says, 'He was an accomplished director. He knew the music, and he knew the instruments. He was very tough on us about learning to play right. But he gave us leeway to do a lot of things."[1]

Phineas Newborn, Floyd Newman, Calvin Newborn, Charles Crosby, and Louis Smith were among my classmates. I played tuba in the band; however, the bass started calling me. And I answered by secretly entering through the coatroom window to practice. A few weeks later, I took the bass home without permission—told mama the school let me borrow it.

One day, I practiced "The Hucklebuck" with the dance band as they rehearsed in the next room. I felt confident enough to join them. So, I walked out with the bass, but the band protested, "Put that bass back . . . you're not a musician."

Phineas Newborn Jr., the bandleader, asked,

"How do you know he can't play? Let's give him a chance."

I played the tune perfectly.

Phineas said, "See, he played the tune right out of the box, yet we had to keep going over it. You're our new bass player."

His statement marked the inception point of my fifty-four-year love affair with the bass.

Eventually, I purchased my first bass with money earned from cutting grass and other odd jobs. My heart pounded with excitement as Dad drove me to Amro Music store. I entered the house, took off the bass case and proceeded to woodshed around the clock. Mama recalled, "I tried to sleep, but your music kept me up. I opened the door, and you looked at me—as if to say, please, don't disturb me. Your haunting stare compelled me to leave you alone."

Dad started taking me to work with him. "If you have a job to do, be on time, and give your best effort," he said. When he cooked, interruptions were taboo, so he requested prior notice on any menu specifications. But one day at the Silver Slipper, the co-owner Mrs. Bloom, violated this caveat by entering his kitchen to suggest some menu changes. Dad took off his chef hat and apron as he walked toward the exit. The owner, Mr. Snooks Friedman, told her to apologize before Dad reached his car. He accepted her apology but tripled his fee.

Dad wanted me to continue his culinary legacy, but I wanted to explore my musical talent. As I was cutting onions and carrots in a small room next to the kitchen, a man came in and asked Dad, "Where's the bass player?" Dad told him, "No musicians work here."

I followed the man outside.

"Excuse me, I play the bass," I said.

"I have a tour lined up, and I need a bass player."

"Are you interested?"

"Yes Sir."

The man was Willie Mitchell, the trumpeter and record producer, who developed hit songs for Al Green and Ann Peebles. Mr. Mitchell assured my folks that he would look after me. And in 1950, I embarked on my second tour—I will cover the first one later—which began in Tupelo, Mississippi and ended in Miami, Florida. We rocked the house in Little Rock, Arkansas. I got excited, spun my bass around and a loose, wooden plank on stage ejected it from the bandstand into the audience; amazingly, the bass and the patrons escaped major damage. The cats in the band laughed about this for weeks. On Miami Beach, I got drunk and passed out. Then the cats covered me up to my nose in sand (the sand stayed in my ears for years). We stayed at the Sir John Motel, and I ran into Blue Mitchell in the lobby. He asked me for five dollars, but my inner voice told me to say no. But I gave it to him anyway, then a few hours later, I heard Blue got busted trying to cop some dope. A fellow band member, Jimmy Ritchie, got drunk and I had my first driving experience: fifty miles from Mississippi to Memphis.

Beale Street produced Jimmie Lunceford, Bill Harvey, B.B. King, Phineas Newborn, Ben Branch, Gertrude "Ma" Rainey, Memphis Minnie, Alberta Hunter, "Lil" Hardin Armstrong, Bill Harvey, Calvin Newborn, Frank Strozier, George Coleman, Louis Smith, Harold

Mabern, and many others. Memphis was a proving ground, so musicians from other cities had to step lightly on Beale Street.

In the Beale Street District, beautiful theaters like the Palace, the New Daisy, the Old Daisy, the Hippodrome, and the Orpheum featured films, plays, concerts, and talent shows. These venues have a history as distinguished as the Apollo, Howard, Uptown, or the Regal. In addition, we played clubs like the Monarch, the Grey Mule, the Tropicana, the White Rose Café, and the Club Handy.

Cotton farmers and workers from Arkansas and Mississippi came out to be entertained after those hot, backbreaking hours in the fields as did the gamblers, hustlers, pickpockets, pimps, and prostitutes. They donned their best suits, picked up their dates, and came out to hear music that uplifted their spirits. On the other hand, some African Americans in Memphis would never hang out on Beale Street. "We don't listen to blues; we prefer classical music," they said. We looked upon them as self-hating imbeciles.

Bill Harvey, the great bandleader and tenor saxophonist, conducted jam sessions and rehearsals at The Mitchell Hotel on Hernando and Beale. Harvey, a demanding mentor who stressed complete musicianship, taught us, "Learn the music in every key." After learning the charts, we invited our friends and family to the gig; on that night, he said, "Take it up a third." And we fumbled over it. Mr. Harvey had lived in New York City and told us, "I saw great musicians in New York hanging on lampposts without work."

Tenor saxophonist, George Coleman: "Saxophonist Bill Harvey had arrangements of everything from '12th Street Rag' to bebop originals like 'Sippin' at Bells' and 'Dance of the Infidels.' Traveling musicians like John Coltrane, who was then working with Earl Bostic, brought their horns to the Mitchell. The result was that there was no jiving at the Mitchell. Coleman points out that the improvisation had to be precise. It had to have all these virtuous elements—good sound, good technique, smooth, clean stuff-well placed. We could play from 9 to 4, and we learned a hell of a lot. You were free to develop your personal style; you just had to have your musical credentials. You couldn't tamper with the standard of the music, pull it down, and it had to be taken seriously or not at all."⁵

One night, trumpeter Benny Bailey came to a jam session with his horn in a paper bag. Bear in mind, we had some great, yet cocky trumpeters like Louis Smith, Booker Little, and Nathan Woodard. First, they laughed at his paper case, and then they called "Cherokee" at a break-neck tempo, but Benny jumped all over it. His solo started way up in the high register then came down low— played his ass off—and earned their respect. Jam sessions gave us a wide palette to experiment and stretch out. We had to play the blues in Memphis to work regularly, but we skillfully interpolated jazz concepts and bebop tunes into our solos. Hungry for knowledge, we studied every style of music; however, the complexity of bebop captured our interest and imagination.

*Sister, Dorothy Joyner Robinson: "I started going with George to nightclubs on Beale Street. The bass was his constant companion: he had girlfriends, but they were secondary and tertiary to his music. He performed at the annual "The Starlight Revue" and "Goodwill Revue" sponsored by the radio station WDIA. Nate D. Williams emceed these shows. We cheered him on. Although our father wasn't a jazz fan, seeing George playing on stage made him proud. Mama had no reservations about the music; she loved it."*⁶

After graduating high school, in 1949, I received full scholarships from three universities. I chose Arkansas AM&N and left home for Pine Bluff, Arkansas. On campus, I remember a posse of sharp young men walking together, Kappas. I asked a brother about joining them, and the next evening he came to my room, dumped out a box of shoes and said, "You are to sort and deliver these shoes to their respective owners by dawn." The next morning, the shoes were still there—that was my answer.

My scholarship required me to play trumpet and tuba in the marching band. Man, marching with the tuba under the blazing Arkansas sun was no cakewalk. I met great musicians like Wesley Westbrooks, Odie Burrus, and Garnett McClellan. Then I organized and led a group of sixteen musicians called the Arkansas

State Collegians, which allowed me to develop my arranging and composing skills. After writing my first arrangement, I burned the midnight oil to copy the parts. The next day, beaming with pride, I handed each musician their part, counted off the song, and a chorus of laughter followed my count. Because the parts weren't transposed correctly. Mr. Harvey's lesson on transposition raised its head once again.

Our music professors wouldn't tolerate jazz on campus, so we rehearsed at night. But our hard work culminated in a victory over the Tennessee State Jazz Collegians in a band competition. Consequently, we won the *Pittsburgh Courier* poll and received an invitation to perform and claim the trophy at a Carnegie Hall concert on April 19, 1952. Fellow poll winners included Lionel Hampton, Billy Eckstine, Nat King Cole, Dinah Washington, Milton Berle, Lena Horne, Clara Ward, and Mahalia Jackson.[7] Unfortunately, the band couldn't perform—the school denied our request for transportation.

Baritone saxophonist, Floyd Newman: "The Arkansas Collegians played dances at both white and black colleges—good music trumped segregation. The school collected the money and paid us only a portion of our earnings. Wesley Westbrooks, an excellent trumpeter and singer in the style of Billy Eckstine, crooned so beautifully . . . people stopped dancing to listen. And Garnett McClellan wrote house-rocking arrangements for the band."[8]

One professor said, "No jazz musician will receive a passing grade in my class, no matter how good they are." This type of narrow-minded ignorance prompted my early withdrawal from college. Upon leaving school, I recorded my first single "Cross My Heart" with the legendary, blues singer Johnny Ace. I was shocked when a few years later we lost this blues giant in a silly Russian roulette game. Shortly after this recording, Phineas began to call me for gigs. Phineas Newborn Jr. reigned as the supreme master among Memphis musicians: a great composer and arranger, and a multi-instrumentalist (trumpet, saxophone, vibes, and bass). He could sight-read complex music perfectly. Newborn went through music teachers like we went through clothes. I remember him drawing upon his photographic memory to transcribe—with minimal labor—the Dizzy Gillespie big band version of "Good Bait" for us, the *exact* chord voicings. When not practicing, he read voraciously. Phineas inspired Memphis musicians like me, George Coleman, Booker Little, Harold Mabern, Frank Strozier, Louis Smith, and Charles Lloyd.

In 1953, Phineas, Calvin, and I recorded two songs (released as 78s) at Sam Phillips' Sun Studio, "How High the Moon" and "Round Midnight." Don Robey recorded Phineas to launch his Progressive Jazz label. Orbiting under the influence of Nat King Cole, who set the pace for jazz trios, we recorded without drums. Moreover, we liked the challenge of playing without drums because it required a keen rhythmic sense. Nat Cole and Johnny Moore's Threeblazers played and rocked dances without drums. In this format, Calvin comped using the Freddie Green style; by the way, Calvin was playing octaves on guitar—before he heard Wes Montgomery.

Meanwhile, I heard bassist Sam Jones with Tiny Bradshaw's band in Memphis: his sound and concept floored me, so I told Sam, "I want to play like you." And he said, "You gotta go to New York to really learn this music." I considered his advice against the backdrop of the virulent racism in Memphis. For instance, I once witnessed racist white men drag an African American man to death behind their car. The racism, the indifference towards jazz, and Sam's statement fueled my desire to leave Memphis.

So, I packed my bags and set out for Detroit. I met Barry Harris, Tommy Flanagan, Donald Byrd, and Sonny Red at the Flame Show Bar, Baker's Keyboard Lounge, Blue Bird Inn, and Crystal Show Bar. The musical fires in Paradise Valley burned around the clock, which made sleeping a snooze and lose proposition. In fact, Detroit had so many great local musicians that securing work, as an outsider, posed a challenge. But my blues education saved me. Landis Brady, a great, blues guitarist with steady jobs, hired me.

The idea of an out-of-town bass player getting steady work pissed off a few local bassists. And early one morning two cats knocked on my door, one of them said, "Come hang out with us." We silently rode to an undisclosed location. When we arrived, I felt a draft—as Prez used to say—from the three bassists in the room: Ernie Farrow, Doug Watkins, and Alvin Jackson (Milt's brother). Doug said, "Go pick a bass," the rhythm section took off into "Cherokee" at one-hundred miles an hour and put the bridge in three-quarter time: eventually, everyone dropped out, except me. A tall man, who silently loomed in the background, finally spoke, "I had nothing to do with this . . . Y'all grabbed the wrong one." His name was Paul Chambers, and we played duets for the rest of the session.

Before I could settle in Detroit, Uncle Sam drafted me. On September 2, 1953, I reported to Fort Jackson, South Carolina. My heart raced and beads of sweat dripped down my face as the bus pulled up to the base. The drill sergeant lined us up and said, "You fucking maggots are now property of the United States Government. We issue commands and you will obey . . . is that understood?"

"Yes Sir!"

Damn! I went from jamming with the baddest cats in Detroit to hot, crowded army barracks in South Carolina. In the early fifties, Fort Jackson became the first army installation to undergo large-scale desegregation. That's why I dealt with racist commanding officers who resented talented African American soldiers. For example, a racist sergeant assigned me to latrine duty, so I quoted the army manual, "According to article so and so, you can't do that." In truth, I had never read the manual, but it worked. Playing Sousa marches on tuba at Fort Jackson was a drag, so I went AWOL to join the Special Services unit at Fort McPherson (Atlanta).

At Fort McPherson, I reported to General Alexander Bolling. I had to rehearse my appeal because failure would have put me in jail: "Sir, I can best serve my country by arranging and playing excellent music with the great musicians under your command. . ." General

Bolling, who felt my sincerity, said, "I will order your transfer if you orchestrate the "Southland Panorama" for a one-hundred-piece concert band and nineteen-piece dance band." With a huge sigh of relief, I accepted his offer. The cats were asking, "How's it going in there?" "Are you gonna make the deadline?" After camping out over a pile of manuscript paper with plenty of black coffee, I completed my arrangement within a week and joined the Special Services unit. The late, great Wynton Kelly and I played "Body and Soul." He said, "You have the sound and feeling I'm looking for," and welcomed me into the small ensemble.

One morning, Phineas called me from Camp Gordon and said, "They always assign me to latrine duty and won't let me touch the piano." I persuaded General Bolling to transfer him to Fort McPherson. I did the same for Louis Smith and "Silly" Willie Wilson.

Trumpeter in the Third Army Band, Willie Thomas: "George was playing in the Army band when we met at Fort McPherson in 1954. I remember pouring cold water on his head to wake him up sometimes. George had a wonderful sense of humor, and we became good friends. He transferred to the Third Army Special Services Unit about a week after me. We performed at Third Army camps throughout the country.

Wynton Kelly and Duke Pearson [played trumpet] were among the musicians stationed with us. In fact, Duke arranged our music. Playing with these great musicians inspired me. General Bolling loved to hear Wynton play in the officer's club lounge. Our unit also had some soon-to-be celebrities like: MC Leonard Nimoy, Dr. Spock; Barry Newman, actor; Ken Berry, F Troop, Mayberry; Wynton Kelly, George Joyner, Louis Smith, Duke Pearson, Silly Willie Wilson, and T-Bone.

Atlanta had some interesting racial undertones at that time . . . good ones. Wynton befriended Walter "Chief" Aiken who built the beautiful four-star Waluhaje Hotel to facilitate trade between eastern white executives and the southern contingencies. They wanted to transcend the strictures imposed by segregation. Chief Aiken asked Wynton to organize a group that included George Joyner and me for weekend jam sessions. The sessions were open to a mixed crowd. And they supported us—standing room only for months. The Chief also hired Paul Chambers, Charlie Rouse, Benny Green, and others to play with us. When Wynton left the Army, it folded. However, the Waluhaje and the American Legion played an important role in the progressive march toward integration.

Quite often, George and I would hit the 'hood' after the gig for some serious ribs and shrimp, and he was always nervous with me on hand. The police were always looking and prodding. For example, one night, my '42 Chevy wouldn't start, so George and I were pushing it. Then the police showed up and started their funny business; I flashed my Army ID and reminded them we were government property—due back at the base. They got the message and helped us push the car. We laughed about that for weeks."⁹

Uncle Sam cut me loose on September 1, 1955, and I joined B.B. King's band. My bandmates included: George Coleman, Evelyn Young, Floyd Newman, Lawrence Burdine (saxophones), Calvin Owens (trumpet), Ted Curry (drums), Millard "Mother" Lee (keyboards), Earl Forest (songwriter and vocalist), Onzie Horne Sr. (arranger), and me (Fender Bass).

Floyd Newman: "B.B. wasn't satisfied with his bass player, so I recommended George."¹⁰

Dorothy Joyner Robinson: "Prior to their first tour, George, Floyd, and B.B. stopped by my apartment in Chicago. George would often introduce me to "famous musicians" as a joke. When he introduced me to B.B. King, I didn't believe him, because B.B.'s shoes were dirty, and his hair was a mess. I thought it was another prank. B.B. and I used to laugh about this encounter. B.B. would have parties for the band members and their families at the Paradise Theater. Mommy and Daddy attended one of these parties and had a ball.

George earned good money with B.B. and purchased a new Crown Victoria for Daddy. One afternoon in Memphis, a racist cop detained us. The officer asked, "How can a nigger afford such a fine car?" Daddy said, 'My son gave me this car as a gift.' I told the officer, "My father hasn't broken any laws and shouldn't be subject to interrogation." Daddy admonished me, 'Never give a racist cop a reason to brutalize you. If he reacted violently to your statement, I would have defended you with my life. It's better to ignore ignorance than become victimized by it.'"[11]

We fulfilled over two hundred one-nighters. One night, we heard Monk Montgomery with Lionel Hampton; he played some house rockin' Fender bass. B.B. looked at me and said, "I want you to get one." Monk, Jymie Merritt, Roy Johnson, John Willie "Shifty" Henry, and I were among the few playing this new instrument.

Blues legend, B.B. King: "In the mid-fifties, I was meeting guys who are very big in the jazz field. George Coleman who was later with Miles Davis, Herman Green, who was with Lionel Hampton, was with me for a time, and so was George Joyner, the bassist."[12] "Some, like George Coleman, were brilliant beboppers. George's ideas flowed; he had a superb knowledge of music and could play anything he heard. With me George [Coleman] would grow restless, and urge me to learn chord changes in modern jazz."[13]

"George Joyner played the blues with the feeling and groove I needed to produce the sound I envisioned for my band. He made a substantial contribution over those six months in 1955."[14]

Baritone saxophonist, Floyd Newman: "Our band had a strong jazz undercurrent. Onzie Horne Sr. wrote Basie-style arrangements, which we played before B.B. came on stage. In Detroit, we opened for Dizzy Gillespie. After listening in the wings, Dizzy made a cameo appearance with us."[15]

George Coleman: "We would go out with B.B. and we'd play maybe a couple of jazz tunes. We had a good book, too. We had special arrangements. There was a great arranger from Memphis that wrote for the band named R.J. [sic] Onzie Horne. We had jazz pieces, too: a lot of original stuff. And we had another singer in the band who would come on, and then after that B.B. would come on. They would become impatient. They'd say, "Hey, come on!" "Where's B.B.?" We were playing all this hip stuff, you know, and they didn't want to hear it. They wanted to hear B.B."[16]

We played in Money, Mississippi on the day Emmett Till's murderers were acquitted. After the gig, the police pulled our bus over. Some of the cats, determine to go down fighting, began loading pistols and shotguns, but B.B. talked to the officers, and they let us go.

One night, B.B. sang "Woke up this Morning," and hit one of those powerful high notes, then fell completely silent, I asked, "B, are you okay?" He whispered, "No, I just shitted myself." He had to slip out to the bus and change.

While playing with B.B., I witnessed a concerted effort to destroy rhythm and blues to pave the way for Elvis Presley, Carl Perkins, Jerry Lee Lewis, and Bill Haley: "This so-called rock n' roll is a direct steal from rhythm and blues, and in the process r 'n' b was slaughtered. Good people went right down the drain. There was a mysterious period that affected many states in the South in 1954-55 during which rhythm and blues was barred from the radio. They said it was race music and was unfit for public consumption ("In December 1954, the Music Publishers' Protective Association passed a resolution condemning "dirty songs" as showing bad taste and a disregard for recognized moral standards and conventions.")[17] As a result, there was almost a boycott against R 'n'B, and during this year you heard none of it on the radio or even in record shops down there. Shortly after this ban, people like Bill Haley and Elvis Presley—who was right there in Memphis, as I was—came on.

Soon they were calling this beat "rock," and it evolved into "rock 'n' roll." In the mad wave that followed this, many rhythm and blues artists were pushed under. It seemed to be a plot to boost rock 'n' roll and certain people. For example, if a rhythm and blues band like Johnny Hayes or Earl Forest, or B.B. King came into the city and no radio station was playing their latest release, it affected their draw." . . . B.B. King recorded the song "16 Tons" in Houston in early 1955. "During the first week of its release it was selling so well it looked like it might hit a million," he continued. "It was told to us that some people came from New York and bought the master record and the singles were taken off the shelves." Ernie Ford's version of the song (recorded in

November 1955) became a big hit. "Anyone who can find B. B.'s "16 Tons" has a collector's item. Also, it was one of the greatest R&B arrangements to come out in years—since the best charts of Louis Jordan's band and Charles Brown's trio."

"You take any good jazz musician who is over 30 and you'll find R&B in his background. Cannonball, Bird, Coltrane, Dizzy, Ahmad, Tadd Dameron, Benny Golson—all put in their apprenticeship with those good bands. These bands were workshops. They played good arrangements. Also, when several bands happened to be in the same city, members would look each other up and have jam sessions."[18]

We fought to get in those rhythm and blues bands—when we left—we had our sound, concept, and feeling. Each band had a different pocket, so you couldn't leave B.B. King's band and go to Louis Jordan's band playing the same way. Joe Liggins, Roy Brown, Sonny Thompson, and Charles Brown had different blues styles. They would change the groove on the drop of a hat, and you were expected to follow. If you didn't, they would throw you off the stage. Out of 340 blues styles, you had to know 300 to work. Lester Young said, "If you can't play the blues, you can't play shit." The Memphis blues gave the Phineas Newborn Quartet a unique flavor that drew the respect and admiration of jazz fans and musicians everywhere we played.

2

GIANT STEP: FROM NASHVILLE TO NEW YORK

"When Joe Segal reviewed the show (Birdland Stars) in Chicago later in the spring of 1957, he claimed that the "most swingin music of the evening had taken place between the first and second performances, when Prez (Lester Young) jammed with Phineas Newborn's bass player just pleasing themselves."

–DOUGLASS HENRY DANIELS

In the army, Phineas and I made a pact to come to New York City together. Therefore, I joined B.B. King's band with one stipulation: my departure would be immediate when he called. Phineas left the army a few months before me and rejoined his father's band. In May 1956, after I played the last set with B.B. in Nashville, Phineas called my room and said "George, I'm leaving for New York in two days." I said, "I will meet you there." I told B.B., "I gotta go." He wished me well and I left. The last word of the previous sentence requires further explanation: I left an eleven-piece blues band in which I played electric bass to play upright bass in a jazz quartet, and I left Nashville for New York City—a giant step in my jazz career.

John Hammond and Count Basie recruited Mr. Willard Alexander to book us. Musicians and jazz listeners eagerly awaited the New York debut of Phineas Newborn. And the sidewalk felt like clouds as we checked into the Americana Hotel. Then we got a quick reality check, Phineas Newborn Sr., who served as our manager, asked Mr. Alexander, for a ten-dollar advance to purchase cold cuts. His meager request surprised me, so I said, "Mr. Newborn, I came to New York to live, not exist. If you cannot negotiate a proper fee, I will return to B.B.'s group." The next day, he received a $1,000 advance; however, his blunder prompted us to seek professional management. Mr. Newborn was a great blues drummer, but jazz wasn't his forte. And Phineas had the difficult task of sending him home.

We played in Philadelphia, Newark, and several other cities; this short tour culminated in an appearance at Basin Street East where we played opposite Kenny Dorham and the Jazz Prophets, Morgana King, and later the Clifford Brown/Max Roach Quintet. Phineas, Calvin, and I were the core unit; however, Kenny Clarke, Roy Haynes, Denzil Best, Ron Jefferson, Shadow Wilson, Philly Joe Jones, Ferdinand Everett, Alvin Stoller, Larry Ritchie, and Kenny Dennis were our drummers. Phineas could play extremely fast, so our group required great drummers. And we hired and fired several who were unable to handle fast tempos. When drummers straggle on up-tempo pieces . . . playing becomes hard labor. I can remember one night at the Café Bohemia, Phineas and Mingus played "Cherokee" so fast, Max Roach couldn't hold it down; he just folded his arms and laughed.

Guitarist, Calvin Newborn: "We had a tight knit group. My brother wrote complex arrangements with intricate bass lines; George not only mastered those lines but colored them with his unique style and concept."[19]

The who's who of great jazz musicians like Lester Young, Count Basie, and Papa Jo Jones came by Basin Street, and the press gave us great reviews. Nat Hentoff wrote, "He [Phineas] has more command of the piano technically than any of his contemporaries."[20]

Shortly after arriving in New York, we opened for Count Basie at Birdland. Basie asked Phineas to play solo piano during the intermission. And let me tell you, he played the keys off the piano! Then Erroll Garner strolled in dressed to the nines. As he took a seat at the bar, several Basie band members began to instigate a piano battle. "Did you hear that, Erroll?" "Wow!" Erroll ordered two double shots of whiskey, sat at the piano, and played a hypnotic riff with his left hand—ba da! bip ba da! ba da! bip ba da—hit a groove that had everyone dancing including Phineas. He blew our minds, because we thought he couldn't outplay Phineas. Wrong! The truth is whenever two masters play opposite each other, whoever plays last takes the trophy.

Our mission, to carve out a niche in a fiercely competitive jazz scene, hinged on excellent performances and reviews. The Editor-in-Chief of *Esquire* magazine wanted an interview, but Phineas, preoccupied with chasing women, ignored the writer's request. So, he asked for my help. I told Phineas, "Man, don't blow this opportunity, we need the publicity . . . talk to him." Thus, he became the first jazz artist featured in *Esquire* magazine:

"I was among the first in town to hear the extraordinary talents of a young man appropriately named Newborn. So far as all the jazz devotees on the scene were concerned, it was the birth of the most exciting piano sound since Bud Powell first appeared, and comparable to the emotion that must have prevailed when Art Tatum first blew in from Cleveland.

As a matter of fact, the experience of hearing Newborn—and I was at Basin Street every night—was strangely similar to the Louis Armstrong and Beiderbecke first weeks: the small group the first night; the word was racing around town that this is "something you've gotta hear"; the increasing number of top musicians dropping in as the week went by; the increasing tempo of enthusiasm; and the ovation of closing night.

Genius is a pretty large tag, and one not lightly tossed around by professional jazz musicians. However, I heard "genius" a lot about this young man that week. The Newborn Quartet (the other members are ace-drummer

Larry Ritchie, bassist George Joyner, and guitarist-brother Calvin Newborn) are definitely a modern group in what might be called the "Charlie Parker tradition." Of course, my reaction was, "How did all of this come out of Memphis?"— which I had hitherto thought of as a stronghold of "rock and roll." It appears unlikely that the obscure young man from Memphis must wait for international recognition; since American jazz is in the ascendency, news of our new talents spreads rapidly to every part of the globe."[21]

This article was a tremendous boost for us. From the outset, Willard Alexander, spoke words that threatened our unity. I sat within earshot of a meeting wherein he told Phineas, "You are paying them too much . . . the people are coming to see you." When the meeting adjourned, I told Phineas, "If you believe what he just told you and cut my salary, I will rejoin King's band." He said, "I would never do that."

On the first recording, *Here Is Phineas*, Atlantic Records used Oscar Pettiford on bass and Kenny Clarke on drums. The record executives hired name-brand artists to promote the album. Phineas wrote bass lines too difficult for Oscar to put together in the studio. I remember Oscar throwing the blackened manuscript paper across the room and yelling, "I'm not being paid enough to play this!" I had already mastered these lines, so I played on several tracks.

In 1957, we joined the Birdland Stars tour and performed with a stellar cast of all-stars that included Billy Eckstine, the Count Basie Band, Bud Powell, Terry Gibbs, Terry Pollard, Sarah Vaughan, Joe Williams, Chet Baker, Zoot Sims, and Jeri Southern. *"The tour began with a performance in White Plains, New York, in mid-February, and then a midnight show at Carnegie Hall that same night, followed by a date in Newark the next day, with another midnight performance at Carnegie Hall that night; the night after that they played Boston. Those concerts marked the beginning of a string of one-nighters that took the performers from New England to New York, Virginia, the Carolinas, back through the Midwest, south to Kentucky, and Missouri, and then north to Chicago, Ohio, Canada, followed by Brooklyn and the District of Columbia out to the West Coast, all in six weeks' time."*[22]

In North Carolina, I fell during a horseplay incident backstage and opened a gash on my head that required stitches, but the segregated, white hospital refused to treat me until I filed a police report on the assailant. One of the cats brought Billy Eckstine over to the hospital, and Mr. B raised so much hell; the nurse called the police. When they arrived, Mr. B pointed in the officer's face and said, "If your mother's head was bleeding like this wouldn't you demand treatment immediately?" The officer told the doctor to treat me. Then someone got word to Bob Redcross, Eckstine's valet, who came and whisked him out of that hospital. Mr. B was a fearless man who would kick anybody's ass—including the police—in a heartbeat. Another incident I remember was when someone told the police we had drugs on the bus. And they threatened to search everyone and everything on it. So, Chet Baker dropped his dope close to some clean musicians. And the police decided to arrest everyone seated near it. The cats told Chet, "We will kick your ass when they release us." After this stern warning, Chet confessed and they arrested him.

The vibraphonist on the Birdland tour, Terry Gibbs: "When we played down South, we used to eat on the bus because they wouldn't let black people eat in restaurants. By this time, I was the only white person left on the show because Chet Baker had gotten busted, Jeri Southern was fired for being drunk, and Zoot Sims had left for other commitments. Some of the guys said, "Terry, why don't you go out and eat? We understand the situation, there's no reason for you to have to suffer." But I said, "forget it," and we used to go into supermarkets and buy cans of tuna fish and sardines and eat them in the bus."[23]

"We traveled by bus everywhere we went, except one night when we chartered an airplane, we weren't sure this airplane could get off the ground, it looked so raggedy. Terry [the late, great pianist Terry Pollard] had never been in an airplane before and was really scared. When everybody in the show found out how scared she was, well we put her on. "It's nothing at all! You get up there and plane goes down, goes up, it goes to the side, it shakes, but don't worry, it's normal." We took off, got up in the air, and we

were flying for about a half-hour when suddenly, we hit an air pocket, and the plane dropped 100 feet. Everyone panicked except Terry Pollard. She was the only one who didn't get scared because we had told her the airplane would do this. She was cool and we were a nervous bunch of idiot's."[24]

I remember the plane flew everyone back east from the West Coast, and a faulty engine had the plane flying on an angle. Mr. Eckstine paced up and down the aisle saying, "This might be it, if you owe cats money, pay them." We landed safely after this horrible flight.

"Once during the Birdland Stars of 1957 tour, he [Joe Williams] visited her [Sarah Vaughan] in her hotel suite in Louisville, Kentucky. Johnnie Garry, Sonny Payne, and Freddie Green with the Basie band were there too. They ordered food from room service; when the waiter brought it to the door and discovered he was serving blacks, the smile disappeared from his face. There was always some incident. It was never a smooth road to progress."[25]

The racial climate in America during this time forced tour manager Al Wilde to include an anti-Jim Crow clause in the booking contract. "Birdland Stars the Broadway package soon to hit the one nighter's scene will not play any hall where obvious biased seating arrangements are in effect."[26]

Calvin Newborn: "George and I sat behind Sarah Vaughan and Freddie Green on the bus. I chaperoned Bud Powell to make sure he was on time. One night, in Montreal, Phineas dug deep and played on that higher sphere. When we came off the bandstand, I saw Bud banging his head against the wall. I said, "Bud, it's time to hit," and guided him to the stage, where he played a soul-stirring rendition of "Like Someone in Love." Billy Eckstine and Sarah crooned like two lovebirds. They reached a new plateau every night. The Basie band featured Lester Young on "Polka Dots and Moonbeams," and man . . .

In Detroit, at the Bluebird Inn, Phineas borrowed Thad Jones' trumpet and blew the roof off the joint. Chet Baker refused to play after him. Hearing so many great musicians perform, night after night, inspired us. When we played at Pep's Show Bar in Philly, the audience, which included

Lee Morgan and John Coltrane, responded with great enthusiasm. A draft notice ended my participation on the Birdland Stars tour. In May 1957, I reported to Fort Dix and therefore missed the West Coast tour. Les Spann replaced me on guitar. "[27]

On this tour, I developed an excellent rapport with Lester Young. He taught me the importance of knowing a song's melody and lyrics: "A soloist should express ideas consistent with a song's theme," he said. When I asked him about Charlie Parker, he took a deep drag off a joint, exhaled a plume of smoke and said, "When I first heard Bird, I asked, 'Who is this little motherfucker coming out of nowhere playing my stuff, their stuff, and his own shit?' "We were proud of that little motherfucker.'"

Mr. Young had a subtle sense of humor. For example, after a gig, he would say, "I got a date with Minnie Five, and she don't talk back."

Finally, I asked, "Who is Minnie Five?"

He held up his hand.

Man, I fell out laughing.

On a serious note, he made a prophecy about the future of jazz: "By the '80s, the music will be scotch and water—mostly water. Then the industry will march the 'great white father' off the mountain to save the music."

After the Birdland tour, we performed as a single attraction again. In Los Angeles, I went out for breakfast, looked across the street and saw Phineas walking with Paul Chambers and Philly Joe Jones. So I follow them to the motel and bang on the door.

"Who is it?" Philly said.

"Open this fuckin door!"

When he did, I saw a belt tied around Phineas' arm.

I said, "Are you crazy?" "That shit will kill you!"

I jumped all over them for trying to turn Phineas on.

Paul told Phineas, "He's telling you right. Heroin addiction is hell. You should avoid it."

I said, "Let's get the hell out of here!"

During this West Coast tour, I composed a song entitled "The Duke of Winds." I gave the tune to Phineas in the dressing room—shared with Toots Thielemans. After our set, the manuscript paper was missing, and the song later resurfaced as "Bluesette" composed by Toots Thielemans. I always wanted to question Toots about this song, but never got the opportunity. When musicians called the tune on gigs, I pled ignorance.

Calvin Newborn: "In Los Angeles, we played at The Composer on Sunset Blvd. The Miles Davis Quintet was working down the street from us, so we stayed in the same motel. Coltrane developed the "sheets of sound" concept from listening to Phineas. He admired my brother's artistry. The Phineas Newborn Quartet was taking the jazz world by storm. We played the Newport Jazz Festival, Café Bohemia, The Colonial Tavern in Toronto, Red Hill Inn in New Jersey, Storyville in Boston, and the Blue Note in Chicago."[28]

In 1956, RCA Victor, whose roster included Elvis Presley, Sam Cooke, and Harry Belafonte, signed Phineas. On October 16–22, 1956, we recorded *Phineas Rainbow*. I wrote and arranged a song called "Clarisse" for this record date; however, when it was released, I wasn't credited as the composer. I published the song with Chaz-Marr, Mingus' publishing company, and he helped me receive proper credit for my song.

The day before flying out West to record with Phineas, I went to Colony Music store. Once inside, I see John Coltrane, humming the melody on a lead sheet, so I snuck up behind him and grabbed the nape of his neck.

"Why are you mumbling to yourself?"

"Get out of my store!"

He turned around and laughed.

"How are you?" "I found a couple of songs tailored made for Phineas."

I mentioned our record date and Coltrane, who loved searching for beautiful songs, suggested the two in his hand: "While My Lady Sleeps," and "Black Is the Color of My True Love's Hair."

Coltrane said, "Phineas has an amazing harmonic concept; you think he's going one way and he goes somewhere else." I took the songs to Phineas, he ran through them and said, "I want to record these tunes." They had to scrap some of the other tunes planned for the session. Coltrane had a high regard for Phineas and vice versa.

The liner notes on *While My Lady Sleeps* captures a moment from this record date, "At the end of every take, the men in the orchestra unanimously applauded Phineas' playing. This, in these hardened days of record-making, is a most unusual occurrence, and a tremendous tribute to the genius of this young inventive pianist."[29]

On March 23, 1958, we recorded our last album for RCA Victor—*Fabulous Phineas*. Phineas was at odds with RCA's vision for his career. Furthermore, the plantation contract limited his control and mobility. And Phineas rejected the terms, because he wanted self-ownership. To that end, he positioned himself to change his record company, booking agent, and personal manager. Suddenly, the other record companies rescinded their offers, and Phineas found himself in New York with no work or work prospects. Roy Haynes and I hired him for a three-week engagement at Birdland; however, they garnished his pay for the first week. And we argued with the owner who then agreed to pay him for the next gig, but Phineas never made it back. He had a nervous breakdown.

If you give a genius a big problem, they can resolve it easily. On the other hand, a small problem can overwhelm them. We insulated Phineas from mundane concerns—spoiled him. He had been independent most of his life and didn't want to be fenced in by RCA or anyone else. Now, he couldn't work here or abroad. The message from the industry was clear: we own you!

RCA gave Phineas a saxophone, a vibraphone, a piano, etc. Phineas thought these were gifts, but they were debts owed to RCA Victor. He offered to pay off the debt. They said, "No, you must stay with us." Phineas rejected the deal and an industry wide boycott followed his decision.

Jet magazine ran the story: *"Jazz pianist Phineas Newborn suffers a nervous breakdown and was confined to Kings County Hospital in Long Island, N.Y. Newborn was ordered by his physician, Dr. Tom Grier to take a 5-week rest due to the strain of a hectic nightclub and theater schedule. The pianist's wife, former Harlem model, Dorothy Stewart, said he would resume work about the middle of November."*[30]

A rumor implicating his wife, Dorothy, as the root cause of his nervous breakdown began to spread, which wasn't true, because she loved Phineas. From this point forward, Newborn's career was a consistent interplay of setbacks and comebacks. The industry spread rumors that he was crazy and difficult, which undermined his career momentum. Phineas wanted to control his career and receive compensation commensurate with his talent.

I had to strike out on my own hoping Phineas would get well soon. Coming to New York with him gave me the credentials to move forward, and I was excited about the prospect of working with other musicians.

3

FREELANCING

We had to look over our shoulders in New York, because great musicians came out of the woodwork. And you had to outblow a cat to earn your place in the pecking order.

—JAMIL NASSER

THE BASS MASTERS

I lived in the Alvin Hotel, across the street from Birdland. And my room served as storage space for fellow bassists: transporting a bass can be physically challenging and stressful. One night, I opened my door, and found Charles Mingus, Oscar Pettiford, and Ray Brown ready to retrieve their basses for work. They played and I heard an incredible display of bass mastery—beyond words to describe.

When I took my first lesson with Mingus, he said, "Put that piece of firewood in the corner," and he sold me a beautiful Gabarielli 5/8 bass. I played it on my Prestige dates and some of the early recordings with Ahmad. Unfortunately, in 1969, I sold it to make ends meet. I came by with Ray Brown's latest record, *Bass Hit.* Mingus grabbed the record, threw it against the wall, drew his hand back, and I warned him, "If you hit me, I will rock your clock." In those days, I was doing two hundred push-ups and sit-ups a day—in peak physical condition—wisely, he backed off. Mingus could be volatile at times.

Mingus shared valuable insights about arco and pizzicato technique. After a lesson, he said, "I have a radio interview; you wanna go?" "Sure," I said. During the interview, Mingus said he could pluck and bow the bass simultaneously. The bass section of the New York Philharmonic called the station and vehemently doubted his claim, so Mingus invited them to his home. I happened to be visiting him that day. I opened the door and said, "Mr. Mingus, doesn't want anyone to say a word to him." Mingus retreated to his bedroom for an hour and came out with his bass and bow. One bassist attempted to ask a question. Mingus said, "Shut up, no talking allowed!" Then he proceeded to play some complex figures using arco and pizzicato technique simultaneously. The bassists sat in awe as he dispelled all doubts. They apologized and Mingus said, "I can teach a junior high student to outplay all of you in three months, now, get the fuck out of my pad!"

I remember Percy Heath bought a new bass and Paul Chambers, Mingus, and I took turns playing it. Suddenly, Paul reached over and took the bass right out of Mingus' hands. "You out-of-tune playing motherfucker!" "How dare you take the bass from me!" I told Paul to apologize, and he did. He got off easy.

The great bassist Oscar Pettiford took me under his wing after hearing me with Phineas and testing my skills. I dropped by the Black Pearl to hear Oscar and the other bassist was a no-show. So, Oscar asked me to play bass, while he played cello. I read the chart down, but the last five bars were missing. When the notes on the paper stopped, I stopped. After the set, he tapped my shoulder and asked, "Why did you stop playing?" "The chart is missing the last five measures." He said, "Use your ears and improvise but never stop. If you make a mistake, you can follow with something that makes the error less obvious. Aside from that, you sound pretty, damn good." I remember Oscar played "Polka Dots and

Moonbeams," and forgot the melody, but he covered himself in such a way—it didn't matter.

In addition to Mingus, Pettiford, and Brown, I studied with Michael Krasnopolsky, a great symphonic bassist and a terrific teacher, who taught me the discipline and practice required to read European classical music.

PAPA JO JONES

Papa Jo Jones' definition of jazz would be banned from most colleges, "If you can't sing to it, dance to it, or fuck to it . . . it ain't jazz!"

I can remember Papa Jo and Lester Young talking about Norman Granz . . . I chimed in, "I don't trust him; he should be closely monitored."

Papa Jo screamed, "What has he done to you?"

Prez said, "That's right, how long have you known the man?" I had no answers and no place in their conversation.

When I came to New York, Papa Jo took a special interest in me. If I asked him a question, he might answer next week or next year. "Don't forsake your southern heritage to be hip, because two hips make an ass . . . keep your mouth shut, listen, and observe." He said, "Industry predators and police have a special radar for vices, so leave your habits at home. And be careful in your consultations, because everyone there—wasn't there: people can be present and absent at the same time." Furthermore, he said, "I will put you in the right cotton patch to pick your hundred." Papa Jo didn't start drinking alcohol until he was forty years old; he was a sober-minded observer.

He had a copy of "Nigger in the Barnyard" a song issued by Columbia Records in 1908. When his cash reserves ran low, he would visit Columbia and flash that record. They paid him—hush money. He kept a money bowl by the door for needy musicians. He taught me, "Never tell another musician what you earn on a gig, because they will picket you," which meant charge less to replace you. He said,

"Young man, in this world, you will invariably see all the wrong people in the right places."

I played with Phineas Newborn and the Mexican pianist Mario Patron at the 1956 Newport Jazz Festival on the afternoon before the historic Duke Ellington concert and witnessed how Papa Jo became Duke's assistant conductor. Sam Woodyard had a hangover, and Papa Jo heard his beat dragging. So, he stood up, rolled up his Wall Street Journal, and pointed at Sam until he reached the stage. Then, he began slapping that newspaper on the stage to help Woodyard keep time. I used to ask if Duke sent him a check for conducting "Diminuendo and Crescendo in Blue."

Paul Chambers and I met Papa Jo at Birdland one afternoon for a discussion. We were drug-free, young musicians, unaware of the traps. He told us, "A white woman will ask you for a date, secretly place dope in your drink or administer it by some other deceitful method . . . one morning, you will wake up feeling sick, and she will present the remedy. After hanging out for couple of weeks, she will disappear, leaving behind a strung-out musician, primed for exploitative booking agents, record companies, and club owners." As Papa Jo spoke, Paul tapped my foot to point out a fine woman with a big ass. But I was raised to respect my elders, so I wouldn't allow him to distract me.

Not long after this meeting, I went to Birdland wearing jeans and a tee shirt and considered myself a lukewarm competitor comparatively speaking, yet a white woman with a pretty face, long blonde hair, and curvaceous figure propositioned me. I took her back to my room and hit it about three times in one session. Afterward, I fell into a deep sleep, only to be awakened by what I thought was a mosquito under my nose, but to my surprise—it wasn't an insect—this woman had a straw full of heroin under my nose.

I said, "What the fuck are you doing?"

"I don't use that shit," and I kicked her out of my room.

A few months after Papa Jo's warning, I was driving Paul to the Café Bohemia. "Can we make a quick stop on the way?" He asked.

"Are you a junkie, Paul?"

"No, I'm just experimenting: I can kick this shit anytime."

I told him, "This is the first and last time I will do this."

"All right man," he said.

Instead of just dropping him off, I decided to catch a set. On the break, I went backstage and saw Miles Davis sucker punch Paul in his face—knocked him on his ass.

Paul said, "Miles, why did you hit me?"

I said, "What do you mean, why did he hit you?"

"Hit him back!"

Paul wouldn't do it.

I told Miles, "Hit me like that," but he wouldn't.

I was angry.

I must jump ahead about ten years from our Birdland meeting to share the following story. When Paul got too high, he would drop by and say, "I'm up on that mountain and can't make it home." I would usually give him my sofa, but one night pus-filled sores covered his arm. I said, "Paul, those sores look bad; my children use the sofa . . . I can't put their health at risk." He said, "I understand," and left. Under the influence of heroin and a junkie, white woman, Paul left his family, became ill, and expired at thirty-three years old in 1969. At his funeral, I leaned over his casket with tears in my eyes and said, "The man warned us about this, but you didn't listen. "Why?" Someone asked me, "What did you say to him?" I said, "That's classified information."

Being young and impressionable, I wanted to hang out with my musical heroes. Papa Jo told me, "Drink hearty, but stay in your party." I was walking down the street with some great musicians, who were dope fiends, and Papa Jo appeared out of nowhere, "Drink hearty, but stay in your party; whichever way they go . . . you go the opposite way." Then he crossed the street, folded his arms, and waited. I obeyed his directive and walked away.

I met up with the cats later and found them lined up backstage, twelve-deep: they each handed this dude twenty dollars and received a small package. I said, "I'll wait for y'all outside." When they came out, I said, "You motherfuckers complain about no gigs and low pay . . . that shit makes y'all easy targets for exploitation, because y'all can't say no."

Those musicians expired years ago, and I am still here. A few junkies lived to see old age but most died young. It all depends on your physical constitution. Heroin and alcohol killed John Coltrane ten years after he stopped using, because his liver worked overtime to filter that poison out of his body.

During those days, Heroin undergirded the jazz economy. For example, I acted like a junkie to record for Prestige Records. I would drop by the studio with my shades on talking like a junkie: "Hey dig, baby, give me a damn record date, Jim!" The subterfuge unraveled when he gave me a bag of dope and followed me into the restroom. In two minutes, my inexperience told on me. "You're not a real junkie, are you?" I said, "No!" And they said, "No more record dates." Clean musicians were ostracized from recordings and gigs, because we didn't need to see the man before the music started or when it stopped.

I often consulted non-addicted associates about their experiences. Bassist Julian Euell said, "I witnessed the devastating effects of heroin, so I never used dope. Moreover, my close friend, the late, great trumpeter Benny Harris, told me, 'If I ever catch you using that shit, I will kill you. Heroin is nothing to fool around with.' Certain musicians didn't hire me because of my non-user status. And I constantly encouraged musicians to stop using drugs. So much so, that they would say, "Julian, we already know what you're going to say." It frustrated me because it took more than words to beat that addiction . . . dope destroyed so many talented musicians."[31]

RED GARLAND

After leaving Phineas, I worked with the late, great pianist Red Garland. I loved his bluesy, swinging piano style, which I heard on his Prestige dates as a leader and a sideman. His brilliance, however, wasn't confined to music. Red, a master etymologist, could break down the Latin origin of many English words. As you will soon read, he was a formidable opponent in debate, stubborn, and persuasive at times. He used to say, "I'll bet you a fat funky monkey, I'm telling the truth."

Red boxed in his younger days. He told me Miles Davis would throw punches and stop an inch away from his face. But one time they hailed cab and Red bent down to get in and Miles caught him with an upper cut to the jaw. Red got up, hit Miles with a one-two combination, left him on the curb, and told the driver to take off.

Our short-lived yet tight working band with John Coltrane and Donald Byrd recorded: *All Mornin' Long, High Pressure, Dig It,* and *Soul Junction. Garland in the liner notes of Soul Junction said, "George Joyner was rather new to me at that date, but he fitted in very naturally"*[32]

I remember Red called me a few hours before a gig and said, "I want you to drive me to Philly; I will run inside real fast . . . then we can drive back in time for the gig." Here, we go again. I told him, "That's absolutely ridiculous."

On the way to the gig; I asked him, "Why do you use that shit anyway?" "It's nothing but poison."

"Don't knock it, unless you've tried it."

At that moment, my curiosity exceeded my good sense. "Well, let me try some."

He pulled out a small package and gave me a few hits. I waited but nothing happened, so he gave me more. I never shot up; I snorted the dope. By the time, we got to the gig, I could barely hold my eyes open and vomited profusely between sets. Moreover, I had to use the piano as a prop to hold me up. I left my car at the club, took a cab home, and was sick as dog for the next three days. I never thought of using that poison again.

FIRED BY SONNY ROLLINS

Sonny Rollins: ". . . In those days, I was not concerned with the niceties of life or refinements. I was trying to get a sound; a certain sound, and did not care what I had to do to accomplish that. I used to hire guys and fire them on the same night. I was pretty ruthless in that respect. You read a lot of stories about that; Sonny Rollins anecdotes about me hiring and firing guys on the same night. But, I had to do it."[33]

Leonard Feather: "Sonny spent weeks at the Vanguard experimenting, toying briefly with the idea of using a quintet. For the first week, he had trumpet, bass, drums, and himself. The second week, he dropped the trumpet and brought in a new rhythm section"[34]

Many jazz listeners are aware of the historic recording *Sonny Rollins live at the Village Vanguard* with Wilbur Ware and Elvin Jones; however, few realize they replaced us. The original group, a quintet, included Donald Byrd, Gil Coggins, Roy Haynes, and me: Sonny Rollins fired us!

Time to hit, 10:00p.m., well, not yet, Sonny is warming up backstage. We're on the bandstand ready to play. At 10:45, he stepped out and played near the entrance door for ten minutes. Then he reached the bandstand at 10:55 and played some more. Finally, we grew tired of posing with our instruments and segued into an F Blues. The crowd screamed their approval.

After the first set, Sonny called a meeting and upbraided us for not respecting his leadership. He said, "I am the leader." "You cats should follow me." Donald Byrd spoke first, "What are you doing?" Sonny said, "You can leave!" One by one, we posed the same question and received the same answer. Rollins fired each one of us and hired Wilbur Ware, Elvin Jones, and Pete La Roca. Our intention wasn't to disrespect Sonny, but we were ready to hit. Rollins is a very creative musician. We used to have long philosophical conversations on a wide range of subjects—the sun rose over a few of them.

Dealing with musicians with different temperaments, attitudes, and habits created challenging and comical situations. For example, Wilbur Ware had a gig, but didn't have a bass. I had an extra one and let him borrow it: I never saw that bass again. And Donald Byrd damn near starved to death saving money to buy a bracelet watch that Miles Davis was sporting that year.

LOU DONALDSON ON JAMIL

"I met Jamil in 1957 through my good friend, trumpeter Idrees Sulieman. At that time, he was still George Joyner. His steady beat, big sound, and ability to swing impressed me. So, I hired him to play on Lou Takes Off, an outstanding record date that created opportunities for me as a bandleader. Just listen to his bass line on "Sputnik" the up-tempo tune I composed based on "What is this Thing Called Love." Then you will know why we had a standing agreement to work together whenever he was available"[35]

Lou studied the whole lineage of jazz saxophone. He would demonstrate the virtues of Earl Bostic, Tab Smith, Willie Smith, Johnny Hodges, and Charlie Parker. I looked forward to playing with him. *Art Blakey and The Jazz Messengers: Night at Birdland* featuring Clifford Brown and Lou is a classic live recording; they made history. His solo on "Wee Dot" is a masterpiece. Lou has the whole ball of wax: great sound, and the ability to swing at all tempos from a ballad to a blazing up-tempo piece. And he can entertain an audience with his incredible sense of humor. I always admired Lou's education: he holds three college degrees. In addition, Lou is a family man, drug-free, and a great businessman.

JAMIL ON MEETING RANDY WESTON

In 1957, I went to see Randy at the Village Vanguard. As I was listening, I began to hear tonal colors that would complement his music. After the set, I introduced myself and said, "I would love to play with you." "I play mostly original music," he said. "I know all of your songs." Shortly thereafter, he called me for a gig. I played his music and thus began our forty-year musical relationship and friendship. We introduced and recorded "Hi Fly" at the 1958 Newport Jazz Festival. Weston's style contains echoes of Monk and Ellington—playing with him prepared me for Monk's bandstand years later.

Pianist and composer, Randy Weston: "I have always been attracted to sound, which is not only extremely important but also difficult to acquire.

Jamil represented the Jimmy Blanton tradition of sound and rhythm. He could get inside the various African styles and meters of my music. "He had a strong blues sensibility and a warm bass sound. In addition, my music has a rhythmic diversity and harmonic complexity that requires big ears: Jamil could hear the music. His solos weren't just a collection of notes and phrases—they told a story.

For example, his solo on "Babe's Blues" is a soulful blues story. Jamil had a strong affinity for the 6/8 rhythm. The album Little Niles encapsulates the chemistry we shared and the attributes of Jamil's playing I mentioned earlier.

I remember Jamil and I played a New Year's Eve gig that drew fifteen people. I said to him, "You can't draw anybody." He said, 'You're the leader of the group; I guess nobody wants to hear you.' We had a good laugh about that gig. "[36]

TALES FROM THE STUDIO

Evans Bradshaw attended Manassas High School with George Coleman and Frank Strozier. Evans ranked about two degrees beneath Phineas Newborn, yet he always tried to outplay Newborn.

For Evans' first recording date, *Look Out for Evans Bradshaw,* Orin Keepnews hired Wilbur Ware on bass and Philly Joe Jones on drums, but Evans, intimidated by their presence, couldn't play. I replaced Ware on bass. And I told Evans, "Cool out, New York is just another city." My advice fortified his confidence enough to make the date.

Producer, Orin Keepnews: "We took this unknown rather nervous young man (understandably awed by his first trip to New York and by coming into contact with jazz musicians that had previously been just names and influences to him) and set him down in a large and imposing recording studio. We provided, for that first album, one familiar face (bassist George Joyner, whom he had known back in Memphis, and one top-grade experienced pro (drummer Philly Joe Jones). It now seems almost amazing that Brad, instead of just falling apart, very quickly stopped being nervous and awed and proceeded to turn out an album that a lot of people found impressively inventive, tasteful, swinging, and enjoyable."[37]

I recorded *The Big Sound* and *Groove Blues* with Gene Ammons. Gene closed his gig on the West Coast, then sold his plane ticket to buy some dope. It looked like he wasn't going to make it. And that's why Bob Weinstock called Pepper Adams, Jerome Richardson, Paul Quinichette, and John Coltrane. Eventually, he arrived by bus—without his horn—so Coltrane gave Gene his tenor and played alto on these dates. Coltrane's gesture of respect impressed me. Gene had a huge sound on tenor sax. I will never forget how he would start his solos from the back of the bandstand, and then take two steps toward the microphone every chorus . . . when he got to the mic, the walls and the bandstand vibrated.

DOWN HOME REUNION

Author's Note: "In the earlier months of 1959, three men from the United Artists Recording Company were speaking with Phineas Newborn about recording an album of music with a "southern" beat, portraying the southern music lover in all capacities. Phineas is originally from Memphis, and with a little pushing on his part, it was decided all the artists should be from Memphis. Down Home Reunion, recorded by these young men from Memphis, is a first-class demonstration of talent in a rare form. In the recording, there are no solos [drums]; however, with his minute musical genius on drums, Crosby goes through the entire selection of tunes with precision and high-class definition of sound and rhythm. This set took all day to cut, and the playing time of the album is approximately 38 minutes. Crosby remarked of this record date in New York in this manner, 'We played a lot and ate a lot.' Most of the tunes are slow, sleepy sounds, reminiscent of the South. However, 'Blue and Boogie,' a Gillespie-Paperelli tune, is one you really wake up on."[38]

SNAPSHOTS

I performed with the late, great poet Langston Hughes in 1958. *The Amsterdam News* published the following review: "Langston Hughes brought his Poetry-to-Jazz uptown Saturday afternoon to Branker's Melody Room where an appreciative audience listened and enjoyed. Hughes read his works to a background of jazz supplied by Raz[sic] Ramirez on piano, Lonnie Coles on drums, and George Joyner on bass. John was the emcee. The program was billed as The Poetry of Harlem to the Music of Harlem in Harlem."[39]

A jazz fan taught me a profound lesson on this gig with Langston Hughes. After we finished a set, he approached me and said, "I really enjoyed your music."

Trying to be hip, I said, "Ain't nothin' happening."

"What do you mean?" "Anybody can do that?"

"Didn't you practice your instrument for many hours to become a professional musician?" If that's your attitude towards your craft, whenever and wherever you play; I will avoid that place." I never saw the man again, but he taught me to value my gift and the music.

Red Mitchell had a brother named Whitey Mitchell: they both played bass. Whitey made some derogatory comments about me. I took my bass to his gig and challenged him to a cutting contest. After I played circles around him, he apologized.

We could walk the streets without fear anytime of the night. They called us the "cooks." In the fifties, we made a good living working exclusively in the African American community, and the people could sing our solos. One night, Stanley Turrentine played a gig in Harlem, and someone stole his horn. The word went out, "Don't get caught with that horn." Stanley was directed to a phone booth in Harlem, and there he found his horn.

When Miles had the group with Cannonball and Coltrane, I wouldn't hang around after my gig, because those two giants had a cutting contest every night . . . an electrifying display of saxophone mastery.

I worked with the great trumpeter Kenny Dorham. We recorded an album with Hank Mobley on Blue Note entitled *Curtain Call.* I remember a jam session with some cats who couldn't play: Kenny got up and played a barrel polka—cleared the bandstand. I loved his sound and concept, but he wasn't satisfied with it. Idrees Sulieman and I stopped by his place, and he opened a drawer full of mouthpieces. He was attempting to broaden his tone by changing mouthpieces. But Idrees told him, "You must spend time with a mouthpiece before concluding whether it's good or bad.

Idrees introduced me to Islam . . . a critical turning point in my spiritual development.

4

FROM THE CROSS TO THE CRESCENT

Nobody was hiring Yusef (Lateef) at that time because of his affiliation with the Muslims. Prejudice against the Muslims was running high in those days. It was difficult for so many African-Americans in the 1960's, especially for anyone associated with the Muslims, who were completely ostracized. So, nobody wanted to hire Yusef, except me, that's how he became my musical director.

—OLATUNJI

I have met many musicians who professed Islam and Christianity. But Jamil lived in accord with the moral guidelines and precepts of Islam . . . always willing to help fellow musicians, students, and elders.

—GEORGE COLEMAN

DIZZY SPEAKS ON ISLAM AND JAZZ MUSICIANS

Dizzy Gillespie witnessed the conversion of jazz musicians to Islam: "Man, if you join the Muslim faith, you ain't colored no more . . . They had no idea of black consciousness; all they were trying to do is escape

40

the stigma of being colored. When these cats found out Idrees Sulieman, who joined the Muslim faith about that time [1947], could go into these white restaurants and bring out sandwiches to bring the other guys because he wasn't colored—and he looked like the inside of a chimney—they started enrolling in droves. [10]

For similar reasons Gillespie himself once contemplated Islamic conversion but hesitated for fear of jeopardizing his career in the recording business, because it was filled with Jewish talent agents, impresarios, and recording executives. "The movement among jazz musicians towards Islam created quite a stir, especially with the surge of the Zionist movement for the creation and establishment of the state of Israel. A lot of friction arose between Jews and Muslims, which took the form of a semi-boycott in New York of jazz musicians with Muslim names. Maybe a Jewish guy, in a booking agency that Muslims worked from, would throw work another way instead of throwing it to the Muslim. Also, many of the agents couldn't pull the same tricks on the Muslims that they pulled on the rest of us. The Muslims received knowledge of themselves that we didn't have and that we had no access to; so therefore, they tended to act differently toward the people running the entertainment business. Much of the entertainment business was run by Jews. Generally, the Muslims fared well in spite of that, because we had some who were Muslim in name only. Others really had knowledge and were taking care of business." [11]

"Dizzy respected his uncompromising Muslim colleagues for two important reasons. First, they were advancing their professional interests in ways never contemplated by earlier generations of musicians. Second, in contractual disputes they refused the traditional forms of manipulation. They not only defied racial segregation but aggressively protected their copyrights as recording artists, and opposed discriminatory pay scales; he admired their self-conscious pursuit of African-American history that contributed enormously to the innovative quality of their music." [12]

Religion and spirituality stimulated my interest as a young child, so I questioned my devout Christian parents concerning the Crucifixion of Jesus and the Trinity concept. And they asked our Pastor, Roy Love (my oldest brother, Rev. James Henry Joyner Jr., eventually

41

replaced Pastor Love), to field my questions. His answers, however, only raised more questions, so he advised me to apply faith where logic falters. The other religions I studied weren't much better.

By 1957, I had concluded that most religions were a collection of fairy tales devoid of reason or reality, then, Idrees Sulieman told me, "The Holy Qur'an is flawless and invites its readers to find discrepancies." Then he gave me a copy, and I attempted—for three days—to find inconsistencies but didn't succeed. Moreover, the universal message touched my heart and soul, so I embraced Islam.

When I converted to Islam, a drastic decline in my work schedule followed. For instance, my phone rang early one morning and the caller said, "Your work load will improve if you reclaim the Joyner name." The industry didn't celebrate the jazz musicians who reclaimed their original identity and were no longer classified as "Negroes." Some Muslim jazz musicians retained their Christian names to sustain their careers. On the other hand, Yusef Lateef, Ahmad Jamal, Ahmad Abdul-Malik, Sadik Hakim, Rashied Ali, Idris Muhammad, Idrees Sulieman, and I legally changed our names and braved the consequences thereof. Time and space won't allow me to enumerate them all.

Idrees Sulieman told me about a confrontation he had with racist police in the Deep South: *"In 1949, I was sitting in the white section of the train, when a police officer put his hand on my shoulder and ordered me to move to the colored section. Without making eye contact, I punched his hand and continued reading my newspaper. This officer told his partner, 'I think we should leave this man alone; he must be African.' They left and I completed my journey without further incident."*[13]

On November 29, 1958, I officially changed my name from George Leon Joyner to Jamil Sulieman Nasser: the *Jewish Daily Forward* published the legal notice.

I wrote my parents a letter explaining both my conversion and new name. They respected my decision, but dad continued to call me George. I recorded and performed as George Joyner until 1964.

Islam was and is monotheistic but not monolithic. For example, the Nation of Islam, the Ansars, the Ahmadiyyas, the Shiites, the Moorish Temple, and the Muslim Brotherhood competed for followers, and I explored each as a student. However, I followed the Sunnah of Prophet Muhammad (Peace be upon him).

While I admired the Nation of Islam's ability to reform drug addicts, prostitutes, and thieves, I didn't agree with some of their concepts and ideas. For example, Yacub's history, Master Fard Muhammad as God incarnate, and condemning white people as devils had no basis in the Holy Qur'an. When I challenged them, the brothers told me, "We aren't allowed to read the Qur'an." Yet they had books and other documentation on the horrors of the Middle Passage, the cases of genocide against the Tasmanians and Native Americans, and other historical atrocities perpetrated by white people that bore witness to their evil nature.

Some Islamic groups wanted to exert an inordinate degree of control over my life, so I opted to stay in neutral territory. I attended the mosque on One Riverside Drive led by a brilliant man and a great Islamic scholar, Dr. Mahmoud Youssef Shawarbi.

In fact, Malcolm X consulted Dr. Shawarbi after leaving the Nation of Islam. By the way, I saw Malcolm end a street riot in Brooklyn. The police shot an innocent African American man. And the riot squad came with their dogs, so we went home and got ours. We had trained them to attack on command. Passive resistance wasn't an option on this day. Christian preachers and NAACP leaders stood on cars asking the rioters to disburse, and the people started rocking the cars. From out of nowhere, Malcolm appeared and said, "Brothers and sisters, go home and calm down. Don't destroy your neighborhood because you're gonna wake up here tomorrow—not the enemy." The crowd respected and followed his directive.

I prayed alongside Malcolm at the Riverside Drive mosque and voiced my concerns about his safety. He said, "Allah will protect me, brother, and no one escapes the inevitable." Malcolm was both sincere and fearless. His assassination hit me hard. I went to the Unity Funeral Home to recite prayers over his body. And the white police captain sent an African American officer over to speak to me. He walked up, adjusted the gun on his belt and said, "We cannot grant you access to brother Malcolm." I told him, "My tax dollars pay your salary . . . your job is to serve me."

I must jump ahead to make the following point. Although Islam de-emphasizes nationalism, the liberation and elevation of African American people concerned me, so I investigated every organization from the Southern Christian Leadership Conference under Dr. King's Leadership to the Student Nonviolent Coordinating Committee, and later the Black Panther Party. I remember going to a SNCC meeting where they gave us instructions on how to cover ourselves from the punches and kicks of angry racist mobs. I left because I believed in self-defense. And I didn't like the idea of putting our women and children on the battlefield.

On the other hand, the Black Panthers talked about blowing up the George Washington Bridge. So, I asked them, "Why aren't you brothers and sisters learning how to build bridges, schools, and housing for our people?"

"After the gun battle with the police, where will you take the dead and wounded?" They had no answers.

One brother said, "We need brothers like you to help us."

I said, "You have no clear aims and objectives to attain real power . . . slogans are no substitute for programs geared toward meaningful change."

I clearly saw a tendency towards extremes—non-violence or senseless violence. Islam taught me to value and promote peace, but it also teaches some enemies must be repelled with force. Prophet Muhammad (peace be upon him) taught against extremism, he said, "The flexible tree bends with the wind, whereas the rigid tree breaks. The middle path is the correct one."

Furthermore, Islam teaches that we own nothing, even our bodies must be returned to the earth from which they came. When I received praise or applause for my music, I silently gave praise to Allah who created my fingers and the oxygen I breathe. My book *The Prayers of Muhammad* has specific prayers of protection for any potential calamity. Those prayers have steered me around and through the hairy situations covered in this text.

Some Muslims believe music is haram (forbidden by Islam). While this may apply to music that encourages wrongdoing, I don't believe the bird's beautiful melodies violate divine law. Yes, I performed in clubs that sold whiskey, but I didn't order a double whiskey at the bar. Muslim jazz musicians attracted people based upon the way we carried ourselves. We represented Islam by precept and example; America isn't a Muslim country, and we had to deal with that.

In my travels with the New York Jazz Quartet, I discovered Muslim countries were not beyond reproach. I saw drunken Muslims stumbling around the Medina in Morocco. Furthermore, I witnessed ineffective and repressive governments in Morocco, Tunisia and Libya. In Cairo, racism reared its ugly head, when a merchant, who thought I was Sudanese, treated me disrespectfully until he realized I was American. Then his attitude changed drastically. I said, "I won't buy anything from you," and left. I also witnessed the bitter and deadly conflict between the Muslim brotherhood and the Nasser Administration.

Nonetheless, Islam played a pivotal role in buoying my spirit as I braved the vicissitudes of life, and if correctly applied I believe Islam offers the path to peace for the individual, the family, the neighborhood, the nation, and humanity.

5

OSCAR DENNARD AND THE NEW YORK JAZZ QUARTET

They met Hamp's pianist, Oscar Dennard, a young genius from St. Petersburg, and the only man, woman, or child in anyone's memory that ever cut junior [Phineas Newborn]. At the grand piano in the lobby of the Mitchell Hotel, the traveling musicians' home away from home, the two boy-sized beboppers battled for over a quarter of an hour with their left hands alone. Oscar started the set with nursery rhymes—he had a way of applying Bach three-part inventions to 'Three Blind Mice.' Calvin: 'After meeting him junior woodshedded all day and went out jamming every night for quite some time.'

—STANLEY BOOTH

HISTORICAL BRIEF ON OSCAR DENNARD

*A*lthough a biographical narrative is beyond our purview, I discovered information about Oscar's early history as a phenomenal pianist, composer, arranger, and vocalist in St. Petersburg, Florida. In addition, this *chapter includes the personal recollections of Jamil and several other musicians who either worked with or heard Dennard.*

In the jazz pantheon, geniuses often languish in relative obscurity, Oscar Dennard, the piano virtuoso, who still commands the respect of living masters like Randy Weston, Ahmad Jamal, Monty Alexander, Harold Mabern, and Norman Simmons, falls in this category. Born in St. Petersburg, Florida on June 13, 1928, Oscar was the first of seven children.⁴⁴ His mother, Florence C. Williams, raised her family in the Fourth Avenue South area.

Oscar attended Gibbs Senior High School. Other Gibbs alumni of note include Bob Cooper Jr., a bassist in Paul William's band; Buster Cooper, a trombonist with Lionel Hampton; Frank Royal, a trumpeter with Buddy Johnson; trumpeter, Idrees Sulieman and tenor saxophonist, big band leader Sil Austin. Sil penned a hit recorded by Bill Doggett entitled "Slow Walk." Sil hired Dennard to play piano for his band."⁴⁵ Oscar earned the most popular student title during his junior year.⁴⁶ And he edited, the Student Voice, the school newspaper.⁴⁷

"In December 1943, a fifteen-year old Dennard contributed special musical arrangements to a play entitled "59ʰ Routine" presented at the Manhattan Casino.⁴⁸ Oscar played and arranged for the George Cooper Orchestra.⁴⁹ The band performed regularly at the Manhattan Casino, the premiere venue for dance music in St. Petersburg. "Oscar Dennard the genius piano player and arranger of the aggregation is still doing his number. His latest arrangement is "Piney Brown Blues."⁵⁰

In 1945, Oscar stood before the choir as the lead vocalist at his graduation ceremony. Then later that year, Dennard played a classical piano solo with the One World Orchestra, which featured great, young musicians from all over the world.⁵¹ He was also a visual artist who had a pastel rendering displayed at the Contemporary Arts Gallery in St Petersburg.⁵²

After graduating, Oscar enrolled in Florida A&M College in Tallahassee and joined the Famcee Collegians' orchestra and glee club. He served as an arranger and soloist in each ensemble. Tenor saxophonist Paul Jeffrey recalls, "Oscar told me that he had already mastered the piano literature required for graduation, so Florida A&M bored him. I played with Dennard at a Small's Paradise jam session. History has been very unkind to Oscar.[53]

In 1950, Dennard traveled to Des Moines, Iowa to perform at the Iowa State Fair. When the fair ended, Oscar remained in Iowa. As a musician who welcomed any opportunity to play, he located two clubs, the Sepia and Billiken, and shook each to its foundations. Oscar met Ellsworth Brown, a local pianist and composer, "Oscar was something very special . . . he played classical music too, and his gifts were considerable. He never made people feel underestimated. I was trying to keep abreast myself. Oscar understood that and he never criticized what I wrote or tried to write."[54]

Pianist Norman Simmons met Oscar in 1950: "I rented a rehearsal studio at Gross Music store in Minneapolis, and I met a saxophonist who raved about a pianist he'd heard. He boldly stated, 'This man is the world's greatest pianist.' I said, "Bring him by tomorrow." He did and I sat spellbound as Oscar Dennard played beautiful interpretations of Chopin and Bach. Then he segued into a version of "Three Blind Mice" that not only moved through every key and style of music conceivable but demonstrated his mastery of counterpoint. Then a woman asked him to play boogie-woogie style piano, which he proceeded to play on a level that I haven't heard before or since. Unfortunately, his recordings with Lionel Hampton don't capture the full scope of his genius."[55]

Many people sleep on St. Petersburg's reputation as a piano town. I heard about great pianists like William "Fess" Clark on Beale Street. As a young musician, Oscar hung out with Clark who encouraged him to learn classical pieces with the left hand only. Oscar said, "At first, I didn't believe I could pull it off but through practice I developed a strong left hand." Oscar mastered the compositions of Franz Liszt at ten-years old, and the news of his ability to play such difficult classical pieces—with the left hand only—reached three German piano teachers, and they flew to St. Petersburg to hear him. "He is a genius," they said.

I have performed with many great pianists: Ahmad Jamal, Phineas Newborn Jr., Dorothy Donegan, Randy Weston, Al Haig,

Wynton Kelly, Red Garland, and Harold Mabern. Oscar Dennard, however, made the greatest impression on me.

In 1948, I embarked on my first professional tour as a substitute for the late, great bassist Richard "Tuff" Green on the Steamer Avalon, a riverboat that ran from New Orleans to Minneapolis. By the way, during this tour, I realized New Orleans isn't the birthplace of our music, because African American music and culture wasn't centralized. The music developed along the Mississippi River from New Orleans to Minneapolis then spread around the country. Oscar Dennard accompanied a vocalist in Leon Claxton's (An African American entrepreneur and millionaire who grew up on Beale Street) Royal American Show in Minneapolis. As I was walking past one of the tents, I heard a cat playing so much piano, I froze in place. The most incredible blues to reach my ears emanated from his fingers. Then he did something that blew my mind: he played the strings inside the piano.

Our second encounter took place the following year, when Oscar came to Memphis and dropped by the Mitchell Hotel. He remembered seeing my awestruck face, because I stood close to the stage in Minneapolis. I said, "I loved what you played . . . never heard anything like it." As we were talking, Bill Harvey called Phineas and said, "I got someone here who can cut you in pieces." Phineas came through the swinging doors of the Mitchell like Wyatt Earp, loosening his trigger fingers, and he found Oscar playing in a laid back, relaxed style, which prompted an "is that all you got" wave from Phineas, who then approached Oscar and asked, "You wanna play some?" Oscar said, "Sure!" Phineas began playing "Sippin' at Bells" with an astounding level of virtuosity. When Oscar took command of the piano, he outplayed Phineas with his left hand. Phineas jumped up and said, "Damn!"

Idrees Sulieman: "That boy is good, but he ain't no Phineas," the crowd said when Oscar put himself on display. Oscar had started out slow, warming up with children's songs and nursery rhymes, before gradually working himself into a flurry of notes. Oscar really swung. Phineas approached the piano, grabbed a hold of a phrase Oscar was playing and started running. When he got halfway up the keyboard, though, a surprising thing happened. Oscar took his left hand, and caught Phineas' more elaborate melody and finished it himself. Phineas did not know what else to do except sit there with his mouth hanging open. The two rivals played duets with the left hand for 15 or 20 minutes and then Phineas gave up. Oscar finished the show. This incident sent Phineas into the woodshed for months."[56]

Blues vocalist and pianist, Mose Allison: "Andrew Sunbeam Mitchell's Hotel was the stopping and jamming place. There are players in Memphis who still remember the impact of visits by the likes of Charles Brown and Oscar Dennard, both classically trained pianists who could play in any key."[57]

When on tour with B.B. King in San Francisco, I heard about Oscar's gig at the Blackhawk. On his off-night, I invited him to our gig, but B.B. had reservations about letting him sit-in. He said, "Oscar, your playing may be too deep for our bandstand." Then someone in the audience yelled, "After Hours." Oscar played the tune with his left hand and the audience of about 1,000 people fell into a hypnotic trance until someone said, "No Shit." Then, they snapped out of it.

One night, Oscar Peterson evoked the wrath of Oscar Dennard. Dennard played intermission piano between Peterson's sets at the Blackhawk. And he introduced himself to Peterson, "Hey Oscar, I've been looking forward to meeting you." Peterson replied, "So what!" Dennard answered his affront on the bandstand. Every night thereafter for three weeks, Dennard rewrote the history of jazz piano. Ray Brown sat transfixed as Dennard played the hell out of the piano.

In 1956, Phineas and Oscar had a rematch in New York. During a conversation with Red Wotton, I said, "I finally found someone who can cut Phineas, and if he loses, I'll pay you two hundred dollars." We jumped in a cab and head to the Red Rooster in Harlem, where Phineas, determined to be the victor, attacked the piano with such ferocity that I doubted Oscar's prospects. We had to push Oscar on the bandstand, but he rose to the challenge and played a cluster of chords that created a sound like the Big Ben clock in London and played a haunting version of "Round Midnight." By the second chorus, Dennard had prevailed once again. Phineas never forgot Oscar and would always name him among his favorites for years to come. Anyone with a cursory awareness of Newborn's technical prowess knows the level required to vanquish him in a piano duel.

Dennard signed a five-year contract with Lionel Hampton in 1953. Oscar's long-term contract restricted his ability to record as a sideman or leader. Lionel and Gladys Hampton exploited him: he wrote compositions and arrangements for which he wasn't paid or given credit. In short, they didn't respect his genius and that upset me. For instance, Dennard wrote an arrangement of Lionel Hampton's "King David's Suite" for a 110-piece orchestra and 17-piece big band. The Hampton band was booked to perform the suite with the New York Philharmonic. Oscar completed this formidable task in three days, without the aid of a piano: he wrote the individual parts first and the master score last.

I canceled all my gigs, meetings, and rehearsals to watch him. He had music paper spread across my living room floor. He made one aisle that led to the kitchen, one to the bathroom, then placed Ballantine ale and a bottle of cognac in each corner. He was singing passages, transcribing them, and laughing. "Man, this is gonna sound great."

The following review sheds light on Dennard's arrangement: "The afternoon's most intriguing selection was an excerpt from Hampton's new 'King David's Suite,' which he wrote after visiting the king's tomb in Israel. Hampton wrote the suite for a 110-piece symphony orchestra, but his 17-piece group was highly successful in interpreting its haunting theme. There was progressive jazz, too. Oscar Dennard, the band's young and talented pianist, performed flawlessly on the late Charlie Parker's "Confirmation."[58]

I convinced Oscar that his talent deserved the wider exposure only a small ensemble could provide. When Oscar's contract with Hampton expired in 1958, he decided to leave the band. We recorded the album, *Golden Vibes,* a week before he left. Hamp wanted to fight Oscar, but I told him to fight me instead. Despite Hampton's restrictions, Dennard secretly recorded a trio album.

A MASTERPIECE AT LARGE

On January 9, 1956, Oscar recorded a trio date for EmArcy Records with Joe Benjamin on bass, and Osie Johnson on drums. Produced by Quincy Jones, it remains a hidden treasure in jazz history. They recorded the following tunes: "Invitation," "What Is This Thing Called Love," "Boplicity," "The Wind" (Dennard), "After Hours," "Bess, You Is My Woman Now," "Three Fabulous Rodents," "Choctaw" (Dennard), "Blues in B Flat," and "Pathos" (Dennard).[59]

I appeal to Mr. Jones, please release this recording as it would fill an important void in jazz history. Phil Schaap, the eminent jazz historian, with a reputation for locating rare recordings, tried to find Oscar's record. Unfortunately, his efforts were fruitless. Phil recalls, "I spent seventeen years crawling around the ceiling in the EmArcy vault looking for this record and couldn't find it."[60]

Joe told me, "We made a perfect record." And Osie said, "Oscar, in pursuit of perfection, erased the outtakes." I told Quincy, "I just buried Oscar . . . you owe me an opportunity to hear his record." He gave me a phone number, which I called around the clock for weeks, no one answered.

I have Oscar's arrangement on "Walkin," which is identical to the version recorded by Quincy. I heard that Quincy had purchased the masters and rented it to arrangers for one hundred dollars a day. When I listen to Johnny Mandel's arrangements, I can hear some of Oscar's chord voicings. I always had good ears and listened intently to Oscar when he composed, arranged, and played.

Oscar felt this record exhibited the full range of his piano skills. One day, a Dave Brubeck record came on my car radio, and we looked at each other. I said, "Are you thinking, what I'm thinking?" Oscar said, "Yeah, he's playing my shit." He wondered if Brubeck had access to his recording because Brubeck was on Mercury Records, and EmArcy was a subsidiary of Mercury.

Randy Weston heard Dennard in 1958: "Jamil insisted that I hear a great pianist he discovered, so I went to see Oscar at the Five Spot. He played good, but I wasn't blown away. After the gig, a waiter from the club invited us to his loft, and Jamil said, 'Oscar, play something for Randy.' Oscar played two-hours of incredible piano; he played Bach with one hand and boogie-woogie with the other. Then he prepared a delicious meal, while dazzling us with his command of seven languages.'"[61]

Trumpeter, Idrees Sulieman: "John Coltrane and Sonny Rollins asked to jam with Oscar one night; they ended up sitting with their horns in their laps listening to that magnificent Oscar play."[62]

"I would tell everybody this was the world's greatest pianist. I told Milt Jackson, Connie Kay, Richie Powell, and Clifford Brown "You want to hear the world's greatest pianist, Oscar Dennard?" Who's Oscar? So they all decided "okay man" and we jumped in a cab and came up to the house and I played the tapes. Richie Powell laid on his back and said, "I thought it was bad enough with Bud Powell and Art Tatum, but this cat, man! Clifford Brown said two weeks before he was killed, "I don't think I ever heard that much piano playing in life again." Connie Kay says, "Yeah I never heard anything like that."

Milt Jackson didn't say nothing. The next morning about nine o'clock Milt calls "Hey, what you doing?" I say "nothing." I got to come back over and hear that 'cause I don't believe what I heard last night." (laughter) He came over and wanted a copy and I said, "No, Oscar told me not to give it out." At that time, Oscar was with Lionel Hampton's band in Europe. Milt got very angry with me about it, that was about '56, and I saw Milt six months ago [1980] in Copenhagen, the first thing he said, "You wouldn't give me a copy of Oscar." I would put him and Bird in the same category. He knew everything and he could play "Confirmation" with the left hand and Chopin with the right, he had that kind of coordination. One time Phineas Newborn was playing in some club on Broadway and Oscar walked in and he stopped playing and said, "Oscar Dennard is in the house." At one time Oscar was playing in Warsaw when he finished he received this note, he looked at it and it said fantastic, (signed) Arthur Rubinstein. So, we rushed down to see what room he was in and they said he just left for Moscow. He could learn a language in five or six weeks."[63]

THE NEW YORK JAZZ QUARTET

Levi Unwine, a friend of Idrees Sulieman, directed a theatrical company, which planned to present an African American cultural extravaganza replete with dancers and musicians. He lined up a tour in Africa, but it fell through. Nevertheless, we had developed a well-rehearsed sextet comprised of Harold Ousley (tenor sax), John Handy (alto sax), Idrees Sulieman (trumpet), Oscar Dennard (piano), Buster Smith (drums), and me. Idrees realized that we possessed the sound and talent to travel overseas as a group; however, Ousley and Handy opted to remain in New York.

Alto saxophonist, John Handy: "I was broke and looking for work, so I went to the Five Spot on a Monday night; the house rhythm section included Phineas Newborn on piano, George Joyner on bass, and Roy Haynes on drums. Idrees Sulieman, Frank Foster, and I played several tunes. Charles Mingus liked what I played and offered me a two-week engagement. In addition, upon the recommendation of Idrees, I worked with Randy at the Five Spot.

Idrees asked me about making the trip to Africa. Shortly thereafter, we met with a Moroccan man about the jazz market there. I briefly considered the offer; however, I wanted to launch my career in New York, and I had a family to support.

I met Oscar Dennard around 1952 in San Francisco; he had an incredible knowledge of the piano and harmony. He played chords faster than most pianists played single notes. He lived with musicians far beneath his level. I remember performing with Dennard at a local jam session, where he sang a fantastic version of "Spring Is Here." Oscar was a genius like Art Tatum.

I heard about his mysterious death. In 1961, I saw Jamil and Buster playing at a theater in Milano; unfortunately, I didn't get a chance to speak with them."[64]

IDREES SULIEMAN, TRUMPET

Author's Note: Idrees Sulieman, the master trumpeter, alto saxophonist, and composer was born in St. Petersburg, Florida on August 7, 1923. Idrees had a vision of being a saxophonist. "Sulieman's strange penchant for the saxophone began in a most astonishing way. One day, at age four, he entered a darkened room of the house and encountered, standing in a corner, a man dressed in a glowing white garment holding a saxophone. The figured beckoned to him and young Idrees cried out, bringing his mother on the run. She switched on a lamp and the vision vanished. No one but Idrees saw the man with the horn. 'From then on, all I talked about was a saxophone, but my father insisted I learn to play piano first. Finally, when I was 13, they were going to buy me a saxophone for Christmas.'"[65] *His father, Leroy Graham, was a music teacher and bandleader. Mr. Graham brought Idrees a trumpet—the saxophone was too expensive—and gave Idrees his first music lessons. "My father taught me how to interpret things ... how to phrase music. He explained how things should be played ... he was a great influence."*[66]

Idrees and Oscar lived in the Fourth Avenue South area and graduated from Gibbs Senior High School. One year after receiving his trumpet, Idrees tested his skills alongside professional musicians. "I never will forget the night that Idrees approached the bandleader of the South Carolina Cotton Pickers," Fess (pianist William Fess Clark) said, "They were a touring big band and Idrees was only 14. He asked to sit in. The man looked at him and said he was too young . . . but if he had the nerve enough at 14 to ask to play with a big band, he would let him sit in. When Idrees finished playing, they tried to hire him. But his father wouldn't let him go."[67]

Idrees joined the Carolina Cotton Pickers in 1941, and then studied at Boston Conservatory. He left school to join the Earl Hines Band. "The year was 1943, the year that Charlie Parker was playing tenor in the Hines band, and then *Dizzy Gillespie* and *Sarah Vaughan* also came aboard. "That was a beautiful group of musicians," Sulieman said the other day in a phone interview from St. Pete. "It was the best time of my life."[68]

Idrees recalls, "I was good friends with Monk when he had the band at Minton's," Sulieman noted, "I lived only four blocks away, and we practiced all day to go there at night and play with all the other cats. It was like a family at that time."[69]

Idrees synthesized the swing and bebop approach to trumpet. As a result, he performed and recorded with Louis Jordan, Benny Carter, Coleman Hawkins, Lester Young, John Coltrane, Gerry Mulligan, Buddy Rich, Max Roach, Gene Ammons, Gigi Gryce, Tadd Dameron, Clifford Brown, King Curtis, and Friedrich Gulda, and Thelonious Monk.

Sulieman loved Raphael Mendez and the vibrato in his tone reflects Mendez's influence. Sulieman had a great trumpet sound and a strong blues sensibility. In addition, he tastefully employed varied articulation, glissandos, and quotes in his solos. He idolized Dub Bascomb, transcribing his solos on "Tuxedo Junction" and "Gin Mill Special." Dizzy Gillespie, Miles Davis, and Fats Navarro also expressed admiration for Bascomb's trumpet artistry.

REFLECTIONS ON IDREES

Lou Donaldson: "The best trumpet player around New York during those times [early fifties] was a guy name Idrees Sulieman. He could play better than any of those guys [Miles Davis/Kenny Dorham]. But he knew he wasn't going to get no gigs because all the club owners were Jewish, so he just packed and went overseas. Back then, the Muslims were out."[70]

Idrees spoke about his challenges in New York. "I spent 16 years in New York," he recalled in 1980. "It was depressing. Sometimes in six months, you'd only have two jobs. I got fed up with not working."[71]

Mary Lou Williams: "Monk, Charlie Christian, Kenny Clarke, Art Blakey, and Idrees Sulieman were the first to play bop. Next were Parker, Gillespie, and [pianist] Clyde Hart."[72]

Jamil Nasser: *"Idrees practiced constantly out of the most technically challenging trumpet method books. He had a book that contained wide intervals difficult to execute on trumpet. He would always drop it on trumpet players to test their sight-reading ability. He went to jam sessions and challenged other trumpeters. Moreover, he would finger the horn for hours."*[73] *The great alto saxophonist, Marshall Royal, taught Idrees circular breathing. And Idrees mastered it. On the album, The Hawk Flies High, he sustains a note for fifty-seven seconds on his composition entitled "Juicy Fruit."*

Trumpeter, Webster Young: *"When I walked in the studio to record Interplay for "Two Trumpets and Two Tenors" with John Coltrane, Idrees looked at me like Ali looked at Frazier before the "Thriller in Manila." I thought to myself, this is going to be a long session. Idrees played his ass off on that date."*[74]

His wife Jamila Sulieman: *"Idrees chewed gum to strengthen his jaw and facial muscles. We were walking down the street and ran into Fats Navarro. Fats told Idrees about some chord changes that he wanted to share with him."*[75]

Coleman Hawkins: *"There's a trumpet player who's not so well known, but who's developing his own way of playing and I'd like to bring him out. He's Idrees Sulieman. He plays an awful lot of trumpet. But he plays too much at times. He needs someone to say, settle down, wait a minute."*[76]

Bob Weinstock: *"Idrees Sulieman to me was a great player. He just never got any acclamation. He's like a virtual unknown today when he was right there, you know. He could play anything. And I used him a lot because whatever we had to do he could knock it off right away."*[77]

EARL "BUSTER" SMITH, DRUMS

Idrees dated and eventually married my cousin Jamila, so he often visited her in Englewood, N.J. One day we started playing duets; I didn't use a drum set. I played brushes on a telephone book. He liked what I played, yet realized I needed more experience, so we hit the jam sessions at Birdland and the Black Pearl. Then I heard Idrees and trumpeter George Taitt play with Art Blakey's big band called the Islamic Jazz Messengers. They blew the joint down, man. Whew!

I developed my chops and nailed down a gig at the Five Spot with baritone saxophonist Jay Cameron and Idrees. Oscar Pettiford would come and listen. He approached me after the gig and said, "Would you like to join my band?" I told him, 'It would be an honor to play with you.' I ran outside to tell Idrees about the offer. Idrees told Oscar, "Don't bullshit this young man." Oscar replied, 'No, I want him in my band.' Oscar's quintet, which included Johnny Coles on trumpet, Sahib Shihab on baritone saxophone, Hod O' Brian on piano, Oscar Pettiford on bass and me on drums, had a longstanding engagement at the Black Pearl.

One night Oscar called "Bohemia after Dark" six times at a lightning-fast tempo, after six false starts; I held down the tempo. Sometimes bassists like George Duvivier, Percy Heath, and Paul Chambers were in the audience.

I remember Idrees played something that Oscar didn't like and he told him, "If you come back on the bandstand, I will kick your ass." Idrees ignored his warning and came towards the stage; Oscar sat his bass down, and Idrees backed off. Alcohol ignited violent tendencies in Oscar. I remember he came to the Café Bohemia with his woman, and she said something disrespectful. Oscar swung at her, she ducked, and he knocked the neck off his bass. Then he went back home to get another bass.

One night, Oscar wanted to play cello, so he asked Jamil to play bass. And this was the first-time Jamil and I performed together (1957). I used to hear Idrees and Jamil with Randy Weston at the Five Spot. Jamil, Oscar, and Idrees were recording and working with great musicians. I wasn't on their level musically, but they patiently taught me the music."[78]

During off periods between tours with Hamp's Band, Oscar stayed at my place. And we met with Donald Byrd to discuss his musical residency in Paris. He told us, "I made two hundred dollars a night," which piqued our interest in traveling abroad. By 1958, Idrees, Oscar, Buster, and I were frustrated with the racism, the drugs, and the exploitative business practices on the American jazz scene. And after some serious soul searching, we decided to explore and exploit the international jazz market.

We accepted a two-month engagement at Au Chat Qui Pêche in Paris. Upon arrival, in February 1959, we met with the club owner, Madame Ricard, who had promised to reimburse us for transportation, but we never saw a franc, dollar, or dime. The picture, included in this text, captures the disappointment in our facial expressions—the first of many challenges—we would face. Moreover, Donald Byrd had overstated his earnings—he only made sixty dollars a night.

We played a radio broadcast (later released as a record) with Lester Young. As we were leaving, Lester said, "Can I have a private word with you?"

"Sure," I said.

"I just peed a pint of blood . . . I don't feel good."

"You should go back to the states." I said.

To expedite his return, we asked a French woman to translate these words to the producer: "Mr. Young wants medical treatment from his physician in America and must be paid immediately after the session." But he said, "No one will be paid earlier than the contract states." Me, Idrees, and Buster picked up chairs and threatened to break up the studio. Thankfully, the police captain called to mediate was a Lester Young fan. Although, we waited for hours, they paid him without further delay.

Buchmann-Moller describes Lester's trip back to the states: "The flight to New York was one long nightmare for Lester, who was in such pain by this time that he bit his lips until they bled. He also began to bleed internally and to vomit up blood. On his arrival at Idlewild Airport (now called John F. Kennedy), he was so ill and weak that Elaine immediately suggested that he be taken to a hospital. Lester would under no circumstances agree on this and instead ask to be driven home to the Alvin Hotel. Once back in his room, he sat in his usual armchair by the window and looked for the last time at 52 Street, Broadway, and Birdland, while he listened to his indispensable records and chased one drink with the next one. From that afternoon till midnight, he drank a bottle of Vodka and most of the bourbon, without eating anything whatsoever.

An hour after midnight Elaine finally rang for help, as Lester, dozing in his bed, began to move his mouth as if he were playing the saxophone. The doctor got there twenty minutes later. Lester died at around 3 a.m. on Sunday, March 15, [1959]."[79]

Our quartet packed Au Chat Qui Pêche every night and the crowd loved our music, but some local musicians, intimidated by our hard-swinging band, registered bogus complaints with the French Musicians union. Also, Kenny Clarke told us about a union meeting wherein they voted against assisting us. In the street, French musicians would drawback their feet as if to kick my bass. We played a one-week engagement at the Blue Note with Lucky Thompson, who wanted us, sans the drummer; we politely declined his offer. After fulfilling our two-month contract, it was time to move on—the next destination—North Africa.

HISTORICAL CONTEXT

"Satchmo Blows Up the World: Jazz Ambassadors Play the Cold War" not only captures the international political environment of late '50s and early '60s but also provides the historical context for the New York Jazz Quartet's experiences:

"Between the end of World War II and 1960, as the United States consolidated its new position as the dominant global power, forty countries revolted against colonialism and won their Independence." Indeed, the story of the tours [State Department Jazz] disrupts a bipolar view of the Cold War and takes us into a far more tangled, and far more violent, jockeying for power and control of global resources than that glimpsed through the lens of U.S.-Soviet conflict."[80]

"The CIA was so involved in behind-the-scenes Middle East scheming that an officer in Beirut wondered if "we'd soon be out of key politicians for CIA personnel to recruit." These included the so-called-million dollar agents who steadily received six figure subsidies." By the time jazz tours began, the CIA had already carried out covert actions in the Middle East, Southeast Asia, and Latin America."[81]

"U.S. officials also sought to rebut charges by non-aligned leaders—specifically Nasser and Nehru—that America's racism and imperial ambitions made a mockery of its claim to lead the free world."[82]

As we checked out of the hotel, Kenny Clarke and group of French musicians came across the street, "Where are y'all going?" "We got a gig in Africa."

Buster recalls, "We boarded the ship in Marseille. And Jamil said, 'I heard we might run into a storm.' And thirty minutes later, black clouds suddenly appeared, and the ship began to violently rock back and forth, huge waves would lift the ship, then, crash it down on the water. I thought we were going down. The violent storm we experienced was a dress rehearsal for the life storms ahead of us."

In April 1959, we arrived in Tangier, Morocco. Having no immediate work prospects, we subsisted on meager rations for weeks. We met the Marley brothers, and they set up an audition at a local casino in Tangier, where we played for two months. During this time, Buster and Oscar embraced Islam: Oscar chose the name Zaid Abdel Hamid Mustapha and Buster chose Abu Bakr Salim. Jazz journalist and photographer, Pierre Bardin, recognized Idrees walking down the street and invited us to perform on Radio Tangier International. The release entitled *The Legendary Oscar Dennard* captured this performance. Journalist, Jacques Muyal recalls, "The recording was made with one single microphone; only one take was made for each number. Many musicians received copies of these tapes . . . Dizzy Gillespie, Randy Weston, Ahmad Jamal, Cedar Walton, Kenny Burrell, Billy Higgins . . . All of them wanted this recording to be issued, and it is only thanks to Mr. Hitoshi Namekata that this release has been possible."[83]

The minister of culture in Tangier—impressed by what he heard—told the American ambassador that he wanted us to perform a concert series for the United States Information Agency. It seemed like a great opportunity until the ambassador told us to accept four white Americans as managers and traveling companions. We clearly stated, however, the New York Jazz Quartet prefers to remain neutral and unattached to any government or private entities. Furthermore, our purpose in Africa doesn't include spying or engaging in politics at all. Then, he said, "If you allow them to join you, it would be of great service to your country." When the local Moroccans heard—we refused to work for the USIA—we received dinner invitations. But the consequences of that decision were both far-reaching and tragic, because we encountered sabotage and other difficulties from that point forward.

In Casablanca, we tore the house down. And the Marley brothers wanted to book us for gigs throughout North Africa. At this point, Idrees assumed the leadership position and made the first of several blunders that hindered our progress. For example, when Idrees discovered the Marley brothers were Jewish; he turned down their offer to book us. Jewish club owners in New York put him on the "Do not call list." Unbeknownst to us, the Marley brothers had a monopoly on bookings in North Africa. Now, we couldn't buy a gig. And we noticed some people following us. So, we left Casablanca like thieves in the night to throw them off our trail. A ship captain, who loved our music, decided to help us, so we placed our belongings in drum cases over a period of days and stored them on his ship bound for Tunisia.

We booked a gig in war torn Algeria, which was risky. However, the gig paid one-thousand dollars, and we had a cash flow problem. We met an African American man named Sadler who claimed to work for the Bourguiba Institute. His gift of food silenced our hunger pangs, and the alcohol provided a reprieve from our precarious situation. The adage, "Beware of Greeks bearing gifts," also applies to African Americans. In an alcohol-induced lapse of security, we mentioned our Algerian concert to Sadler. He said, "I can secure the work permits." It sounded good to us, so we agreed. The next day, Sadler drove us to the airport, and we boarded the plane in good spirits eagerly anticipating the concert. At the airport, immigration officials detained us for twenty-four hours without explanation, denied our visas, and put us on a plane back to Tunisia. Idrees told everyone not to resist. But Oscar disregarded his warning. The police picked him up and carried him on the plane. I looked out the plane window and watched as a baggage handler broke the neck of my bass.

HISTORICAL CONTEXT

Who was Sadler? Why did he omit critical parts of the visa application? We must consult history to answer these questions.

During the early sixties, the newly independent African nations were forced to choose sides in a Cold War whose outcome depended on access to and control of Africa's mineral resources. In fact, President Nasser and Lumumba threatened American interests by seeking assistance from the Soviet Bloc. Lumumba's assassination transpired a few months after the New York Jazz Quartet left Africa.

The Peace Corps, Operation Crossroads Africa, and other "cultural exchange" institutions were fronts for the CIA. In fact, Louis Armstrong's appearance in the Congo served as a weapon of mass distraction.

"When Louis Armstrong and his band embarked on their 1960–61 tour of Africa, he like most all Americans was unaware that CIA director Allen Dulles had transmitted an order in late August from Eisenhower to the CIA station in Kinshasa in the Belgian Congo: the recently elected Prime Minister Lumumba was to be eliminated."[84]

David Stafford commenting on a newsreel about Armstrong's visit to the Congo in 1960 said: "As the newsreel narrator notes, the political climate in the newly formed Republic of the Congo was turbulent at the time of Armstrong's visit." But here's what he doesn't share: "During a secession crisis in the newly independent Katanga Province, a day-long truce was called so that both sides could attend Armstrong's performance. Armstrong later commented that he had stopped a civil war."[85]

"The late Edward R. Murrow in a documentary entitled Satchmo the Great said in the Cold War, "America's Secret weapon is a blue note in a minor key."[86] Another weapon was the Central Intelligence Agency: "The CIA's crimes against the peoples of other nations are too numerous to record here in any detail. In places like Latin America, the CIA used military force, terror, and sabotage to bring down democratically elected governments and install right-wing dictatorships that were friendly to American corporate interests. It has infiltrated and fractured the trade union movements of other nations. It has funded secret armies and death squads and destabilization campaigns. It has been involved in the assassination of popular activists and heads of state."[87]

A comprehensive study of jazz and international politics is beyond our purview; however, a basic grasp of the late '50s and early '60s geopolitical context will help us understand the challenges facing the New York Jazz Quartet.

We returned to Tunisia perplexed about our deportation. And after making inquiries, someone told us that Algerian authorities found Sadler's card in one of our passports. Unfortunately, Sadler had been deported from Algeria for spying.

At this point, a serious quandary beset us and our inability to communicate by phone or letter didn't help. Buster functioned as the band secretary and collected contact information from club owners, musicians, and patrons who appreciated our music. We chose six addresses from his phone book, drafted a letter explaining our plight and had a fan send it.

A club owner in Marseille, France, sympathetic to our plight, offered plane tickets and a two-week engagement at his club, The Cave. We delighted audiences' night after night with great music. During our engagement, we met Marcel, a wealthy Frenchman, who offered us a four-week engagement at his club in Aix-en-Provence. We stayed in his family's castle.

When Art Blakey and the Jazz Messengers were late for their appearance at the Opera House, we opened the concert. During the intermission, Lee Morgan began nodding off as I talked. Before his head hit the table, I elbowed his ribcage and said, "Lee, I don't like junkies." He said, 'Man, I'm just experimenting.' While I respect Blakey's artistry, I never liked how musicians join his band clean only to leave addicted. He would cop the dope in New York and tell the cats, "This ain't New York . . . the dope is more expensive here," then pocket the extra money.

One evening several tapes disappeared from our collection, and Marcel confessed to stealing them. We left France to play concerts in St. Gallen, Zurich, and Bern, Switzerland. In St. Gallen, Oscar and I heard a pianist practicing, so we entered the room and took a seat. One of us coughed and he turned around. Oscar said, "Those thirds you were playing are difficult." The man said, 'You play piano?' "Yes, my name is Oscar Dennard.'" The other pianist was Warren Theau. He and Oscar played together for hours. During the rest periods, they discussed exercises that if played incorrectly would cause permanent injury. Warren was so impressed with Oscar; he invited the Swiss Orchestra to come from Geneva to hear us. The club was so tiny, they had to listen in small groups.

After the gig, Oscar and I went to a jam session and heard a saxophonist, who to my ear was terrible, but he said, "Yeah! Man! Blow!"

I said, "What are you talking about?"

"He sounds terrible!"

Oscar said, "I hear where he's going and if he gets there—he's going to be a bitch!"[88]

In 1960, we played at Fatty George's, a popular club in Vienna, and word began to circulate about us. One night, after a gig, a group of Polish students invited us to perform in Poland. We performed at the Club Hybrydy in Warsaw as well as five other cities. The CIA agents didn't follow us behind the Iron Curtain.

Author's Note: In April 2003, Adam Markowicz, the Polish jazz pianist, appeared at a panel discussion on the New York Jazz Quartet. Adam had purchased the recent issue of the Jazz Forum magazine (Polish) with an article and picture of the New York Jazz Quartet: the article pointed out how the New York Jazz Quartet not only played but also taught aspiring Polish jazz artists. Whereas other jazz artists played and left. Adam pointed out, "I have met pianists all over Poland, who remember Oscar Dennard and spoke about his great left hand piano forays. They never heard a pianist do that before."[89]

We softened the Iron Curtain with the love and power of our music; after six months in Poland, we boarded a train for Moscow.

JAZZ IN RUSSIA

Author's Note: I would like to pause here to discuss important historical points concerning jazz in Russia.

The book Satchmo Blows Up the World by Penny Von Eschen documents the relationship between jazz and international diplomacy.

However, the chapter entitled "Getting the Soviets to Swing," documents Benny Goodman's Soviet tour bereft of any historical context thereby reinforcing the myth that he introduced jazz to the Soviet Union:

"Benny Goodman became the first jazz musician to tour the Soviet Union for the State Department, making thirty appearances in six Soviet cities from May 28 through July 8, 1962."[90]

Although, Goodman's tour was the first State Department sponsored Soviet Tour, several African American musicians performed there prior to Goodman.

I recently watched the Russian-American Jazz Summit, a symposium on jazz in Russia. The principal speaker, Cyril Moshkow, who is the editor of the Jazz Ru web site, made the following statement: "The last American jazz band to perform in the Soviet Union until 1953 was a band with Sidney Bechet led by Sam Wooding. The next huge impact was Benny Goodman, in 1962, between these two events there was no direct influence of American jazz music in terms of seeing how it is done."[91] The previously mentioned statement reeks of historical revisionism.

The following paragraphs highlight the contributions of African American artists to Russian jazz history.

In 1926, the first African American jazz band to perform in Russia was Benny Payton's Jazz Kings featuring Sidney Bechet. They spent several months performing in theaters and ballrooms in Moscow, Kiev, Odessa, and Kharkov. The same year Sam Wooding toured Russia with a mixed band, which included African-American musicians.[92]

In June 1959, Dwike Mitchell and Willie Ruff played and taught at conservatories in Leningrad, Moscow, Kiev, Yalta, Sochi, and Riga. Jet magazine did a feature article entitled "Mitchell-Ruff Duo upsets Moscow Conservatory students," "Into Moscow's straight laced Tchaikovsky Conservatory last night wandered two American Negro 'tourists'—Dwike Mitchell and Willie Ruff—better known to jazz enthusiasts as the Mitchell-Ruff Duo. Their casual offer to play for Russian students was accepted, a hall was arranged for the concert and when the 'tourists' had finished the greatest stir in cultural circles since the appearance of Van Cliburn had been created. Hours afterwards 400 or 500 wildly enthusiastic students were still discussing the performance."[93]

Willie Ruff summarized the reason and result of his visit to the Soviet Union as follows: One afternoon, a Yalie came running toward us out on the beach, waving a New York Times he'd miraculously found somewhere in Yalta. On the front page was an article about our Moscow performance. Once we got back to the States, we discovered that the Times story had brought more interest in us than we could believe. Suddenly, every TV producer, club owner, and concert agency wanted us.

Seymour Krawitz, a young press agent Bill Doll had trained, called Dave Garroway and got us on the Today Show, the Tonight Show, an appearance on What's My Line. We were Hot.

But that wasn't why we had gone to the Soviet Union. We had gone, I suppose, mostly because it was there. We wanted the experience of visiting a foreign country that had been sealed tight to American modernism. And it all worked out beyond our wildest dreams. We had given some Russians an 'Opening' to a part of our culture they had known nothing about—to the music that had been invented in America and had evolved in amazing ways over the years. That we were the first jazz ambassadors to the Soviet Union since the 1920's—well, that was our gift to them."[94]

The following year, July 1960, the New York Jazz Quartet arrived in Moscow. We performed at clubs, private parties, and official functions.

A jazz fan who attended the performance told me that Benny Goodman made a speech about the honor of being the first jazz musician behind the Iron Curtain. And a jazz historian in the audience stood up and said, "You are the third, the Mitchell-Ruff Duo was first, and the New York Jazz Quartet featuring Oscar Dennard was second." After the correction, he just counted off the tune and started the concert.

Idrees recalls, "Listeners [in Moscow] were amazed at Dennard's piano ability, and a famous teacher was brought in to hear him. "We were jamming," Sulieman remembers. "But after a while we stopped the jam session. Oscar started playing Chopin, different things like that. The teacher was sitting there with tears coming into her eyes. She said, 'There's got to be something wrong with America. I never heard of him before. And they sent Van Cliburn here. They should have sent him.'"[95]

A representative of the Bolshoi Ballet wanted our group to accompany them; the income and benefits made the proposition attractive. But the offer came with one serious stipulation: we had to denounce our U.S. citizenship in Red Square. Everyone, except Buster, agreed to meet the stipulation, but the deal was an all-or-none proposition. Yet the Russian government offered to send us anywhere in the world: we chose Cairo, Egypt.

EGYPT AND THE CIA

In the early 1960s, Egypt under President Gamal Abdel Nasser's leadership grappled with an internal struggle with the Muslim Brotherhood who wanted to overthrow Nasser and establish an Islamic state. In addition, he implemented land reforms to raise the standard of living for Egyptians.

The United States and the Soviet Union competed for political influence in Egypt. Nasser received assistance from the Soviet Union for the construction of the Aswan Dam.

"The CIA had supported Nasser at first, handing him millions, building him a powerful radio station, and promising him American military aid. Yet the agency was taken by surprise by events in Egypt, despite the fact that CIA officers outnumbered State Department officials by about four to one in the American embassy in Cairo.

The biggest surprise was that Nasser did not stay bought: he used part of the $3 million in bribes that the CIA had slipped him to build a minaret in Cairo on an island in front of the Nile Hilton. Because Roosevelt and the CIA could not come through on their promises of American military aid, Nasser agreed to sell Egyptian cotton to the Soviet Union in exchange for arms. Then, in July 1956, Nasser challenged the legacies of colonialism by nationalizing the Suez Canal Company, the corporation created by the British and the French to run the Middle East's man-made maritime trade route. London and Paris roared with outrage."[96]

"Egypt's ruler Gamal Abdel Nasser was complaining—not for the first time, and not without cause—that the agency was trying to overthrow his government."[97]

The CIA followed Malcolm X in Cairo. Prior to addressing the African Summit on July 23, 1964, Malcolm contracted a severe case of food poisoning and narrowly escaped death. Moreover, the same year, Malcolm, barred from France, realized a powerful force beyond the Nation of Islam mobilized against him.[98]

Bear in mind, how Algerian officials denied visas to the New York Jazz Quartet . . . a powerful force was operating against them as well.

Before leaving Moscow, the Egyptian ambassador advised us to stay under the auspices of the government as opposed to operating independently. We flew to Cairo on August 5, 1960. Shortly after arriving, we met Abdel Magid, a local entrepreneur, who recruited his son to manage us. From September 1 thru 30, the quartet worked at Mena House. Then, we secured an engagement at Lappas, a coffee shop in Cairo; we were booked from October thru June.

In addition, the ambassador wanted us to tour with the King Tut exhibit on an international basis. This deal would have made us ministers of culture representing the Egyptian government; the offer included a good salary, benefits, and dual citizenship. Moreover, they wanted to send us on a nine-month Asian tour to play two shows a week for 250 dollars per show plus extra fees for television appearances. But Idrees asked for more money and thus evoked the ambassador's indignation, who then ripped the contract in half and said, "Mr. Idrees, you are the oldest and should be wise enough to recognize an equitable arrangement." The expression "penny-wise and pound-foolish" encapsulates Idrees' negotiation skills.

Idrees created a similar problem for us at Lappas by sending for Jamila (his wife) to join the group as a vocalist. He told the owner, "She's as good as Sarah Vaughan." In truth, she wasn't qualified to sing with us. The club owner deeply resented the deception.

Dennard would often open or close a concert, especially, when we needed a yes. He never missed except once. Oscar had gone out alone—we never let him do that before—to test some pianos. He left healthy and in good spirits. But, he returned with blazing eyes and a high fever. Several hours later, we left for the gig at Lappas. On the first tune, Oscar missed a few notes, which raised a red flag, because he never missed anything!

"You, all right?"

"I feel terrible!" He said.

We canceled the performance.

Oscar's skin was discolored and pain wracked his body. We sent for a doctor, who said, "It's a mild flu; he will be up and about in a matter of days." I said, "If he doesn't show signs of improvement in a few hours; he's going to the hospital." Oscar's condition grew worse, so we called an ambulance and took him to Embaba Fever Hospital in Giza. The previous doctor misdiagnosed Oscar. Dr. Mustapha Fahmy Khamis said upon seeing Oscar, "Any competent doctor would know he has typhoid fever: it's as common as a cold here." We gave Dr. Mustapha the name of the other doctor. He said, "That doctor has been living in London for ten years . . . his name is listed so friends and family can contact him. I will attempt surgery, but if I see any typhoid ulcers . . . his survival chances are slim to none."

Everyone returned home under intense duress to wait; then a man knocked on the door, "Your friend is gone." Oscar Dennard, the great pianist, expired on October 22, 1960 at 5:30 a.m. He was thirty-two years old.[99] The official cause of death was typhoid fever and intestinal perforation.

Oscar told us he drank a Coca-Cola at the piano shop. Maybe the soda contained the virus? Dr. Mustapha indicated the amount of typhoid in his system would have killed an elephant. And his inoculation against the disease wasn't sufficient to conquer it.

Our grief and our lack of funds for a proper burial made a bad situation worse. In fact, we buried Oscar with two infants on his chest at Zain El Abidin Cemetery. Meanwhile, Sabir Masood told us, "I will never repeat this statement if asked, but your friend was murdered."

In short, the CIA neutralized the strongest link in our chain, Oscar Dennard, as retribution for not cooperating with them. Oscar's death haunted me throughout my life, because I convinced him to join us, and as such felt the pangs of survivor's guilt. This journey was my idea, yet he paid the ultimate price.

I spent hours sharpening my razor. I wanted to kill Idrees, because he had enough money to defray the cost of Oscar's medical care and subsequent burial. In fact, I intervened when a pickpocket attempted to rob him. In Morocco, a man reached in his pocket and I said, "Idrees, he's got your money," and he beat the man's hand until the cash fell to the ground. Idrees would have spared no expense to maintain his health, but he wouldn't help Oscar.

Buster hid my razor, because he knew I was angry. Idrees dropped by and mentioned something about more gigs and our future as a unit. When I said no, a scuffle ensued, and Buster interceded to keep the peace. The New York Jazz Quartet was now history as was our sojourn in Cairo.

Buster and I decided to go to Italy. Our last check from an Egyptian television special barely covered ferry passage to Genoa, Italy: only eight cents remained in the coffers. Our mouths watered when a ferry merchant waved a delectable, giant, glazed donut mounted on a stick like a lollipop—the twenty-cent price tag was too much for us.

We walked in town and found a pawnshop. I offered to pawn my bass, but the owner said, "No, you'll need that bass." "What else do you have?" So, Buster sold one of his ride cymbals for the equivalent of one-hundred U.S dollars, which was enough to buy our tickets to Milan.

We asked someone "Where's the nearest jazz club?" When we arrived, Helen Merrill sang before a packed house. I had worked with her in the Adirondack Mountains. After a glowing introduction, Helen called us up, and we played for dear life. And they booked us for a two-week engagement and gave us a cash advance.

In the fall of 1960, Milan, Italy became our headquarters. However, opportunities to perform in other parts of the continent emerged.[100] For instance, Helen hired us to play in Beirut, Lebanon: *"I took along George Joyner and Buster Smith, which was very nice,"* said Helen, *"but we couldn't find a pianist so we had to use the pianist of the casino. He wasn't really a jazz pianist, and it was amusing. He used to perspire. He tried very hard, but it was very difficult for him. But it worked out all right."*[101]

Tenor saxophonist, Buddy Collette: "I went to Italy for the first time in March 1961. What a trip that was. In one month, I did four albums, including one with La Scala String Quartet, composed twenty or thirty songs, did a TV show in San Remo, some movies, and many concerts. Most of what I did there was never seen or heard back here, but it was a good move to go over there. It was a great experience meeting a lot of the players and working with Romano Mussolini, George Joyner (who later changed his name to Jamil Nasser), and Buster Smith. George and Buster were stranded over there. They had been playing with a musician [Oscar Dennard] who had died suddenly. It really worked out for everyone, because they needed work and I needed a group. It was a great trip, all music for a month. I was getting three or four hours of sleep at night, but I didn't feel tired. I was on top of the world."[102]

While in Milan, we met Flavio Ambrosetti, a local saxophonist, who invited us for jam sessions at his home. Moreover, we recorded several albums together.

We played the soundtrack for the film *Disordine (Disorder)* by Franco Brusati, the distinguished Italian filmmaker. Moreover, Buster and I played a special concert at the San Marco Theater that featured saxophonists Barney Wilen, Flavio Ambrosetti, and Jacques Pelzer, guitarist Franco Cerri, and pianist George Gruntz.

The Italian journalist, Gain Mario Maletto: "The trio that opened the evening was annihilated due to the exceptional virtuosity of two blacks, bassist George Joyner and drummer Buster Smith."[103] The concert was recorded and is entitled "Franco Cerri International Jazz Meeting."

John Lewis came to Milan harboring a romantic interest in Helen Merrill and resented our musical relationship and friendship. John wrote the soundtrack for *A Milanese Story*. And Helen allowed me to eavesdrop on their phone conversation, wherein she asked him why he didn't use me on the soundtrack. He told her, "I don't think he can read music." His answer surprised me, because John observed me conducting a small ensemble that supported Helen and heard me discussing the score with the musicians. John hired Buster to play drums on the soundtrack.

George Gruntz, the great Swiss pianist and bandleader, and Joachim Berendt booked gigs for us throughout Europe. Joachim organized our German tour with Eric Dolphy. We performed in Baden-Baden, Frankfurt, and Berlin. In Berlin, we played on a television broadcast—later released as *Berlin Concerts*.

Buster on *Berlin Concerts*: "Jamil didn't like the date with Eric. When I toured Europe with Sun Ra, many people asked me about this record. For example, Jimmy Woode, the great bassist, came to my hotel in Paris at four a.m. raving about this album."

Vocalist, Lillian Terry:"I remember George as a gentle, humorous young man with a total passion for music. His wonderful personality made him good company. The brief period that I worked with George Gruntz and Buster Smith was a very relaxed and happy one. When we recorded The Four of Us in Milano, the door opened quietly and my friend Helen Merrill accompanied by the four elegant musicians known as the Modern Jazz Quartet entered and waved us on as they sat down. We recorded the four tunes under their benevolent gaze. After the session, we had lunch together. [104]

I recorded an album as a leader called *The George Joyner Quartet* that featured Jacques Pelzer on alto sax and flute, Maurizo Lama on piano, and Franco Mondini on drums. In addition, Buster and I supported Fortunia, a beautiful lead dancer for the Folies Bergère in Paris. "Haitian Fortunia, sensational 18-year-old dancer, has been appearing in the Folies Bergère's first new review since the war, called C'est de la Folie (It's Madness). Fortunia is the daughter of a Haitian father and a blonde Polish mother. Reared in Poland, she was thrown into a Nazi concentration camp during the war. She was liberated by Tan Yanks." [105]

The Katherine Dunham Dance Troupe wanted us to accompany them on a tour, and a German concert promoter, Horst Lippmann, wanted us to tour with Coleman Hawkins and Roy Eldridge. But we were road worn and homesick. Buster and I returned to the United States on February 5, 1962. Idrees Sulieman decided to stay in Europe. The New York Jazz Quartet spread musical joy and love on two continents. We were successful despite many obstacles and challenges. The album entitled *The Legendary Oscar Dennard* provides a window into our unique sound and concept.

Above Left: Jamil's paternal grandmother Betty Joyner. Above right: Jamil's paternal grandfather Andrew "Cap" Joyner.

James Henry Joyner Sr. at work.

James Henry Jr., George, Marjie, and Dorothy, circa 1934.

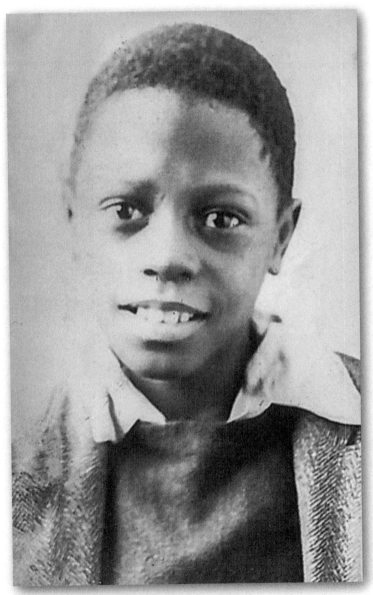

George Joyner, circa 1942.

Front left to right: James Henry Jr., Claude, James Henry Sr., and Helen. Middle left to right: Dorothy, Lois, Ester, and Williametta. Back left to right: Jamil, Phillip, and Charlie, circa 1970. The oldest child, Marjie, and the youngest, Troy are absent from this photo.

The B.B. King Orchestra photographed at the Hooks Brothers Studio on
Beale Street October 6, 1955. L. to R.: George Coleman

*Left to right: George Joyner, George Coleman, Floyd Newman with
baritone Sax, Lawrence Burdine, alto sax, and Calvin Owens on
trumpet, circa 1955. Two unidentified musicians in the back row.*

Left to right: Phineas Newborn Jr., Phineas Newborn Sr., Mother Rosie Lee Newborn, her younger sister Marie, her cousin Bernice, and George Joyner. Blue Note Club in Chicago, circa 1957. Courtesy of Calvin Newborn.

George Joyner directing the Arkansas State Collegians circa, 1952. Used with permission from the University of Arkansas at Pine Bluff.

From left to right: George Joyner, B.B. King, and George Coleman, circa 1955.

Jamil, Fortunia, and Buster, Milan 1961.

Helen Merrill and Jamil in Milan, 1961.

Buster and Jamil in Milan, 1961.

Jamila Sulieman, Buster, Jamil, and Idrees in Cairo, 1960.

First album as a leader in Milan, 1961.

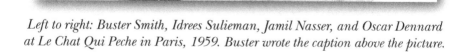

WE FOUND OUT
THAT WE WOULD NOT
BE GETTING THE
AIR FARE TO FRANCE
REIMBURSED

Left to right: Buster Smith, Idrees Sulieman, Jamil Nasser, and Oscar Dennard at Le Chat Qui Peche in Paris, 1959. Buster wrote the caption above the picture.

Oscar Dennard holding court with fans, circa 1960.

Jamil and Idrees, 1959.

From left to right: Idrees, Jamil, Marcel, Oscar, and Buster, circa 1959.

From left to right: Buster, Oscar, Idrees, Jamil, and two unidentified children in Poland, 1960.

Jamil, Ahmad, two unidentified fans, and Chuck Lampkin, 1964.

Jamil and Ahmad, circa 1969.

Left to right: Jamil, Azzedin Weston, Ahmad, and Frank Gant, circa 1973.

Ahmad, Jamil, and Azzedin, circa 1973.

Paramaribo,　June　1967.

Dear Brother,

AS SALAAM WA ALEIKUM.

How are you? Yesterday I got a letter from JAMAL, which I have already answered.

I hope that everything is well now.

It wasn't a pretty experience you get in Surinam, but insah'ALLAH next time you'll be my guest in Surinam. ~~Try to make it to get soon in Surinam.~~ Then I'll let you see my very interesting country and make you get in contact with all MUSLIMS here. Then you yourself will see that JOEMRATIE is the only GANZEER we have.

I think that Mr.LIM A PO, your lawyer, has already start with the civil case. In criminal he, so far as I know, hasn't start yet.

Please don't forget to get me in contact with Muslim organisations in America and Muslim countries. I've write about this also to Jamal.

I hope you'll still remember my plans ,which I have discussed with you.

The day your federation and ours can work together will be e big day. Please discuss this in your federation and other Muslim organisations in your country.

Will you write soon ?

As Salaam

M.S.A. Nurmohamed.

M.S.A. Nurmohamed
Pranchepanestraat 16,
Paramaribo - Z.
SURINAM

Letter from Suriname, 1967.

*Left to right: Al Haig, Jimmy Wormworth, and
Jamil Nasser at Columbia Records 30th Street Studio New York City, 1977.*

The People of Memphis invite you to meet some people from Memphis...

Saturday

Prince Gabe & The Millionaires

Big Sam Clark & Band

Grandma Dixie Davis

Mose Vinson, Sonny Blake & Jeff Grayer with Ma Rainey, II

Mud Boy & The Neutrons (Jim Dickinson, Sid Selvidge, Lee Baker, Jimmy Crosthwait & others)

Sleepy John Estes & Hammy Nixon

Roosevelt Sykes with L.T. Lewis & Wilbur Steinberg

Charlie Banks & The Beale Street Originals with Little Laura Dukes

Furry Lewis

Coon Elder-Brenda Patterson Band with Johnny Woods

Calvin Leavy

Rufus Thomas

B.B. King

Sunday

Rev. James A. Jordan, Pastor First Baptist Church Beale Street

Rev. Robert Wilkins Lane Avenue Church Of God In Christ

Barbara Perry & the New Era Baptist Church Choir

Nancy Anderson with Honeymoon Garner & Fred Ford

Carla Thomas with the Olivet Missionary Baptist Church Gospel Quartet

Rev. Al Green & The Full Gospel Tabernacle Choir

Honeymoon Garner Trio

Herman Green & The Green Machine with Joyce Cobb

George Coleman & Frank Strozier

Sonny Criss

Andy Goodrich & Edward Lewis Smith

Phineas Newborn, Jr., Jamil Nasser, Fred Ford & Calvin Newborn

Nathan Woodard, Calvin Jones & Harold Mabern

Finale With All Artists

Beale Street Productions, 525 Commerce Title Building, Memphis, TN 38103

Appearing at the Memphis in May-- Beale Street Music Festival, Saturday, May 14 & Sunday, May 15, at Beale & Third, near Handy Park. Adm. $2. each day

Program from the first annual Beale Street Blues Festival, May 1977.

Memphis Area Chamber of Commerce

February 18, 1974

Mr. Jamil Nasser
778 Main Street
New Rochelle, NY 10805

Dear Mr. Nasser:

Reference is made to our telephone conversation of February 15, 1974.

I checked with Mr. Puckett to determine what had ensued as a result of your telephone call to him a few weeks ago. Since I was out of town, he assigned the task of raising the money to a committee of Memphis businessmen. Unfortunately, they have been unable to find the sponsors for the considerable amount of money required.

It is regretted that we cannot provide the monetary requirements out of our budget. The concept you have for a show is great if it could have been worked out.

Sincerely yours,

Hugh Nelson, Staff Vice President
Convention and Tourist Bureau

HN:jg

c: Clifford Stockton, Manager, Business Resource Center
Memphis Area Chamber of Commerce

Letter from Memphis Area Chamber of Commerce.

JAZZ FOUNDATION
OF AMERICA

1200 BROADWAY
SUITE 7D
NEW YORK, NY 10001
TEL: 212-213-3866
FAX: 212-532-6519

May 2, 1994

President William Jefferson Clinton
The White House
1600 Pennsylvannia Avenue
Washington, D.C.

Dear Mr. President and fellow musician:

We are seeking your participation on behalf of one of our most important national treasures, Mr. Eli "Lucky" Thompson, a great tenor saxophonist who along with Messers. Louis Armstrong, Charlie Parker, Dizzy Gillespie, Miles Davis, Lester Young and many other great artists founded this great American national treasure known to the world as "jazz."

We are an organization whose main focus is geared to the great living American jazz artist. We are servicing their needs through the Jazz Musicians' Emergency Fund that reaches out to them with passion and compassion according to their needs; financially, medically, musically and spiritually with emphasis on preserving their dignity. It was brought to our attention that Mr. Lucky Thompson, 70 years old, has been a homeless person for more than 15 years, living in the streets in Seattle, Washington and suffering from the usual health problems that are part and parcel of that situation. We want to emphasize that Mr. Thompson has always been totally free of any substance abuse and is a man of great pride.

If you would be kind enough to mention his tragic situation in one of your public appearances, it would make it easier for us here at the Jazz Foundation of America to create a dignified existence for him and many other jazz treasures who are in various degrees of difficulty.

With your help, Mr. President, we are hoping to get the attention of our fellow Americans. Many of our great jazz artist men and women have been the most neglected. It would be a very patriotic thing to reach out and assist them.

Thank you in advance for your time and consideration.

Sincerely,

Jamil Nasser
Vice President

*Letter to President Bill Clinton on behalf of Lucky Thompson.
Used with permission from The Jazz Foundation of America.*

JO JONES

A Love Letter to

Friday, April 23
from 11pm
Village Gate

160 BLEECKER ST (AT THOMPSON) 475-5120. $10

MAX ROACH, ELVIN JONES, GRADY TATE, PHILLY JO JONES, ART TAYLOR, HANK JONES, JAMIL NASSER, GEORGE COLEMAN, DOC CHEATHAM, MILT HINTON, RON CARTER, JOE NEWMAN, MEL LEWIS, CHICO HAMILTON, IDRIS MUHAMMAD, HAROLD MABERN, RAY BRYANT, RICHARD WYANDS, JIMMY ROWSER, EDDIE LOCKE, RAY MOSCA, WALTER BOLDEN, DAVE BAILEY, SHELTON GARY, FRANK FOSTER, HAROLD ASHBY, RUFUS REID, BILL PEMBERTON, JOHN ORR, MANY OTHERS!

COORDINATOR: COBI NARITA/UNIVERSAL JAZZ COALITION, INC.. 924-5026.

UNIVERSAL JAZZ COALITION, INC.
Nobuko Cobi Narita, Director

in collaboration with

THE KINGS SERIES
Jamil Nasser, Director

presents

"GIANTS"

A 2-Day Tribute to the Late Great

REDGARLAND

Friday & Saturday, June 29 & 30, 1984

CHUCK WAYNE QUARTET

LEE WILHITE & THE JAMIL NASSER TRIO

PHINEAS NEWBORN, JR.

LOU DONALDSON QUINTET
in a reunion with BILL HARDMAN

GEORGE COLEMAN QUARTET

THE NEW YORK BASS VIOLIN CHOIR
Bill Lee, Ron Carter, Lisle Atkinson, Michael Fleming, Leon Dorsey & Guest

A BASS BALL: MAJOR HOLLEY & JAMIL NASSER

HAROLD VICK

CLIFFORD JORDAN

Jazz Center of New York
380 Lafayette Street (at Great Jones/E. 3rd St.) - 3rd floor
Ofc.: (212)924-5026; Center: (212)505-5660 (from 1 hr. before performance)

Left to right: Harold Vick, Ricky Ford, Frank Wess, George Coleman, and Sal Nistico. Shootout on Eleventh Street, 1979.

Left to right: Ray Mosca, Jamil, and a partial view of Sal Nistico. Shootout on Eleventh Street, 1979.

Universal Jazz Coalition, Inc.
presents

The Great "SHOOT-OUT ON ELEVENTH STREET"

featuring the Fastest Tenors in Music

GEORGE COLEMAN   FRANK WESS   SAL NISTICO
(Memphis, Tenn.)   (Kansas City, Mo.)   (Syracuse, N.Y.)

HAROLD VICK   RICKY FORD
(Rocky Mount, N.C.)   (Boston, Mass.)

with

JAMIL NASSER   TOMMY FLANAGAN   RAY MOSCA
Bass   Piano   Drums

MONDAY, JAN. 15 - 8:30 P.M.

"Shoot-Out" arranged by Jamil Nasser, Jayeed Festivals

THIRD STREET MUSIC SCHOOL SETTLEMENT

235 E. 11th St. (Bet. 2nd & 3rd Aves.)
Presented in Cooperation with the Third Street's Jazz/Rock/Latin
Department

General Admission: $4   (212) 924-5026 — (212) 777-3240   UJC Members,
Students & Seniors: $3

UNIVERSAL JAZZ COALITION, INC./JAZZ CENTER OF NEW YORK PRESENTS

JAMIL NASSER & FRIENDS

in a
Tribute to the Late Great

HAROLD VICK

"A Song of Love"

featuring our famous "Shoot–Out" with

George Coleman   **Frank Wess**

Junior Cook   **Jimmy Heath**

(Harold was an original member of the "Shoot–Out")

Special Friend
Ms. Abbey Lincoln

and

Harold Mabern   **Frank Gant**

Guest of Honor
Ms. Delores Brinkley

Net proceeds benefit "Save Classical Jazz Art", of which Harold was an originating member.
Tax-deductible donations, in the name of Harold Vick, may be sent to UJC, c/o Cobi Narita.

SAT., FEB. 6, 1988
2 Sets from 9 P.M. – $10.

UJC's 1987-88 8-Concert Series celebrating Late Great Black Artists
is supported in part by a generous grant from the New York State Council on the Arts

JAZZ CENTER OF NEW YORK
380 Lafayette Street (bet. Great Jones St./E. 3rd St. & E. 4th St.)
New York City 10003 - (212) 505-5660

Left to right: Cybill Shepherd, Jamil, and Fred Ford, circa 1979.

Left to right: Aliyah, Umar, Zaid, and Muneer, circa 1975.

Left to right: Muneer, Zaid, and Jamil at Hempstead High School, 1982.

Zaid Nasser and unidentified drummer, circa 1990.

*Left to right: Jamil Nasser, Ernest Ranglin, Monty
Alexander at Ronnie Scott's, 1981.*

6

CHUCK'S COMPOSITE

In 1962, Chuck Bruce, an accomplished model with many friends in the fashion and entertainment industry, opened Chuck's Composite, a chic restaurant on 303 East 53rd Street. Chuck asked me to organize a trio. So, I hired Ronnell Bright on piano and Buster Smith on drums. One night, Ronnell offended Chuck by hitting on his girlfriend, so Chuck asked me to fire him. I told him, "You decided to terminate him . . . you should tell him." Ronnell left and I began searching for a replacement: Bu Pleasant, Herbie Hancock, Barry Harris, Harold Mabern, and Duke Pearson were among the pianists I hired. Duke, however, became the regular pianist. A couple of hours before the gig, Duke called me and said, "I can't get a flight out of Atlanta in time to make it." I called him on the carpet for the last-minute cancellation and began looking for another pianist. I called Richard Wyands. He played flawlessly—problem solved.

I met an up and coming songwriter who respected my musical knowledge and taste. He played his music for me during breaks and after the gig. I encouraged him to continue writing. And he became one of the world's most popular songwriters—his name—Burt Bacharach. Mel Torme, Jerome Richardson, and Papa Jo Jones were frequent visitors to the club.

One evening, I came to work and a union representative asked me, "Why are you using drums?"

"I heard specific rhythms when I arranged my music."

He said, "Chuck's Composite is too small for drums and therefore in violation of the cabaret laws. I was sent to padlock the club."

I told Chuck, "Listen to the man but don't challenge him."

He told Chuck, "On the strength of the bass player's hard work and good attitude, I will help you resolve this problem." Chuck redesigned the club and brought it up to code.

One time a man named Pete was on a date and forgot his wallet. So, I gave him one hundred dollars to cover the bill. He was mob connected, and I used his contacts to extricate a fellow musician from a drug case. This cat got caught sniffing cocaine outside someone's apartment—the police happen to turn the corner. Pete asked me to research the judge assigned to the case, which I did, and my friend beat the case.

At Chuck's, I met an advertising executive from Benton and Bowles, and we discussed my desire to produce commercials. I had musical thoughts that didn't belong on a jazz bandstand. Unfortunately, the African American musical director felt threatened and blocked me.

Chuck's Composite was where Ahmad Jamal heard me for the first time. He had the awesome task of filling a bass chair once held by Israel Crosby. Leading a trio at Chuck's enabled me to redevelop my capabilities as a musical director.

Jamil meets Monty Alexander

Pianist, Monty Alexander: I was born in Kingston, Jamaica, on D-Day, June 6, 1944. My parents recognized my musical talent and paid for piano lessons.

When Eddie Heywood appeared in Jamaica, my father took me to see him. I had studied two of his signature songs, "Canadian Sunset" and "Soft Summer Breeze." After the concert, we went backstage, and I played both songs for Mr. Heywood. He loved what I played, which made my father proud.

In 1963, I came to the United States to play at Le Bistro in Miami accompanying a vocalist on Fender bass. One night, Frank Sinatra and his friend Jilly Rizzo came to the club. We met and they loved my music. After that gig, I flew to Las Vegas for a piano gig. Once again, Frank and Jilly were in the audience. When I finished the set, Jilly hired me. His club, Jilly's, on 256 West 52nd Street, was a favorite gathering spot for celebrities and musicians in the '60s.

Now, I needed a drummer and a bassist. The bass represents the foundation of a band: a building without a strong base will eventually fall. I grew up listening to the great bass players such as Arvell Shaw, George Duvivier, Milt Hinton, Major Holley, Ray Brown, Bob Cranshaw, and George Joyner.

My trio's at Jilly's included bassists Peck Morrison, Bob Cranshaw, Major Holly, Tommy Williams, and George Joyner; drummers Ray Mosca, Al Harewood, and Mickey Roker. Yes, he was George Joyner when our association began. George and I established a good rapport on and off the bandstand.

George had an afternoon audition with Ahmad Jamal before playing with me at Hugh Hefner's Playboy Club. The late, great trombonist Kai Winding functioned as the musical director. Kai hired me, and I hired George. The club didn't possess a cabaret license, so I couldn't use a drummer. Of course, beautiful cocktail waitresses moved about serving customers. Dick Gregory and a newcomer named Steve Martin appeared in the comedy room. George and I performed as a duo, and when we hit a groove, sparks flew.[106]

I can remember when George changed his name to Jamil Nasser. Jamil had a big sound, solid rhythm, and when he played a solo . . . he told a story. His solos made me laugh and shake my head in wonder.

7

JAMIL MEETS JAMAL

Jamil was from Memphis and he was with me ten years. He had a truly fine ear. He came to New York with one of the most profound players in our history, and that's Phineas Newborn. He also worked with Oscar Dennard, who the world does not know about, but he was one of the finest pianists in the world. He toured Africa with him so he was a pioneer in the fullest sense of the world. He worked with B.B. King, and I think he did three hundred and sixty-four one-nighters in one year with B.B. King. Jamil was a giant.

—AHMAD JAMAL

I met Ahmad Jamal, in 1948, when he came to Memphis with the George Hudson Orchestra. Jamal wanted to hear our local legend, Phineas Newborn. And they crossed paths at the Mitchell Hotel, the jazz and blues hub for traveling musicians and local Memphis talent. The pianistic virtuosity displayed by these two eighteen-year old young men was incredible. Their meeting was more of an information exchange session than a piano battle. The shared influences of Art Tatum, Earl "Fatha" Hines, and Nat King Cole shined through, but they had different conceptual approaches. Ahmad lost track of time and was thirty-minutes late for Hudson's concert at the New Daisy Theater.

I heard Jamal's trio with Vernel Fournier and Israel Crosby at the Pershing Lounge in 1958. Their cohesion and perfection compelled me to ask Israel if I could sit in. He said, "There's no sitting in . . . this isn't a jam session." Israel played great bass lines with an ingenious rhythmic sensibility. Too many bassists sleep on his greatness, because he didn't take solos. Bass players can learn a lot about line construction, swing, and taste from him. I remember seeing Ray Brown with an excited gaze in his eyes listening to Crosby. In fact, Benny Goodman wouldn't work sometimes unless Israel was available. After joining Jamal, I couldn't listen to Israel because his perfect bass lines made a deep aural impression.

Ahmad came to New York looking for a bassist to replace Richard Evans, and Philly Joe Jones recommended me. He found me leading a trio at Chuck's Composite. In early 1964, I joined his group. Chuck Lampkin replaced Vernel on the drums. The album *Naked City Theme* captures us live at the Jazz Workshop in San Francisco on June 26–28, 1964. The late, great jazz writer and historian Norval Perkins wrote the liner notes: *"Now that there is a "new" Jamal—all that was so attractive before is still here—only the emphasis has shifted. The shift is due, in no small part, to his new sidemen: drummer Chuck Lampkin and bassist Jamil Sulieman. Lampkin, formerly with Dizzy Gillespie, has a crisp sound and a hard- swinging beat. Sulieman's sound, deeply vibrant, is cleanly articulated and he has that "walking" beat. Both men are capable of producing the varying dynamics and shadings that Ahmad's conception demands. One thing more! Here is a tightly knit group. Each tune, subjected to any number of possible attacks, is spun out with increasing ingenuity and excitement. Within this diversity, always there is the unity of a trio performance, rather than simple piano-with-rhythm backing."*[107]

John King of Melody Maker wrote: "His new unit made an impressive debut in London in 1964. Penetrating the marrow with hammered chords and lightning arpeggios, Jamal's approach was distinctly powerful. Bassist

117

Jamil S. Nasser deftly simplified the pianist's themes with resonance and wit while Chuck Lampkin's explosive cymbals emphasized the new direction. Clearly, Jamal had shown his teeth. His sidemen carefully chosen for their own incisiveness and authority were prototypes for future developments.[108]

Vernel rejoined the trio, and we recorded Jamal's composition "Extensions," which features me and Vernel alternating solos. On July 28, 1965, we performed with the Cleveland Pops Orchestra. The violinist and composer Joe Kennedy Jr., conducted the world premiere of his "Suite No.1 for Trio and Orchestra" written especially for this concert and "Extensions."[109]

Ahmad Jamal: "Extensions" has occupied my thoughts considerably. This is a flag waver every time we play it. We did it with the Cleveland Orchestra. This is definitely 'thinking music.' Ever since we started playing 'Extensions,' it hasn't failed to overwhelm the audience to the point of standing ovations."[110]

Journalist, Ralph Gleason: "Jamal has made each number the trio does into a kind of concerto in which the piano doubles back and forth as a solo instrument and leader of the ensemble. Fournier's ability to keep the drums firmly in place and his masterful control of dynamics is enhanced by his ability to make a series of tones from the drums into a melodic line with the low tuned tom-tom as the bottom note. The bass solos are becoming an important part of Jamal's music. An important part of the remarkable swing this unit projects is due to Nasser's playing."[111]

One night, at the London House, Oscar Peterson came to hear Jamal. In 1959, Oscar had leveled a questionable criticism about Ahmad's style in *DownBeat* magazine. When I looked at Jamal's face, after he spotted Peterson; I knew it was on—the O.K. Corral. Oscar took a seat close to the bandstand. And Jamal proceeded to play the keys off the piano, double octave thirty-second note runs, arpeggios from low A on up, contrary motion sweeps, triple back flips, somersaults, and some other unusual ornaments that defy explanation—left me and Vernel in the dust. We just stood up behind our instruments and listened, which reminded me of an Art Tatum performance I saw in Minneapolis, where John Collins and Slam Stewart let Art have it . . . just stood and listened. The look on Oscar's face reflected shock and awe. Sam Jones (Oscar's bassist) said, "Ahmad, I never heard you play like that." In truth, we were equally surprised.

We recorded two more albums, *Rhapsody* and *Roar of the Greasepaint*. Then Vernel broke his foot in a bicycle accident and had to wear a cast, so Ahmad and I carried him—musically speaking. When his foot healed, Vernel joined Nancy Wilson's band.

In 1966, Frank Gant auditioned for the drum chair: "Ahmad heard me with J.J. Johnson in Chicago and invited me to audition. I played after Jack DeJohnette. And the chart for "Extensions" spilled over the music stand onto the floor; I couldn't sight-read it. Yet Ahmad and Jamil liked my approach and accepted me as the new drummer. My debut in Milwaukee was a baptism by fire. Unaware of the mental and physical demands of Jamal's bandstand, I was drinking, womanizing and these indulgences undermined my stamina. No empty seats were visible as we walked on stage, Jamil picked up the bass, I sat behind the drums, and Ahmad called an up-tempo number, played the melody, one chorus, then pointed at me, "Frank, you got it." Then, Ahmad and Jamil left the bandstand and took front row seats. Man, I fumbled through a thirty-minute drum solo; sweating, dropping sticks . . . couldn't play shit, when I finished; you could hear a rat piss on cotton, no applause. After the set, I told Ahmad, "You don't have to pay me for tonight." And they laughed at me. I felt like a fool but learned a valuable lesson that night: Jamal's bandstand requires a high level of concentration. Ahmad and Jamil maintained a peak performance regimen that included eating health food, exercising, praying, and getting proper rest. I made sure that never happened again—overnight rehab—didn't touch alcohol for the next ten years." [112]

Frank checked out of the hotel we shared and moved into a known party spot with loose women, drugs, and alcohol. He probably got busy with two or three of the women. Frank came to work reeking of weed and booze and stumbled on the bandstand. He couldn't play anything. Man, we almost split our sides laughing at him.

I had a similar experienced at the Village Gate; during the break, I smoked some Chicago-light green marijuana. Ahmad sensed something different about me and reharmonized "Poinciana." Now, I had played this tune well many times, but he lost me . . . put me in a harmonic maze. Frank is right: Jamal's music demanded a high level of concentration.

In April 1967, Don Morrison reviewed the trio's performance in Minneapolis: "Every performer has his ups and downs and—without knowing whether Jamal has had any downs recently—it is obvious that he is having one of his most elevated ups right now. Among other ingredients in the mix is a fruitful rapport with his sidemen, Frank Gant and Jamil S. Nasser. The former is a youthful drummer who occasionally becomes overly intrusive in volume but who plainly enjoys Jamal's fullest approbation. The latter is an intense and musicianly bass player who knows exactly what he and the other two are up to at all times and who seems to supply an entire orchestral accompaniment on his lone instrument." [113]

John King observed, "Ahmad's present combo (Frank Gant on drums, Jamil Sulieman on bass) has had a tremendous impact on American audiences and critics alike (its ironic early doubters now recognize his "improved technique!"). Together since 1965, the trio has crystallized the new mood and bears little resemblance to the '58 edition." [114]

Why did I stay with Ahmad for twelve years? I wanted to see if there was an endpoint to his genius. He could climb to the mountaintop every night, so each performance was an adventure that challenged my musicianship. I received my Ph.D. in bass from him.

For example, he would give us a harmonic sketch of an original or standard, and the song would evolve on a nightly basis. I constructed my bass lines to support Jamal without intruding upon his creative flow. He conducted using hand signals and would turn corners unexpectedly. If someone erred, we took introspective inventory between sets. No talking or greeting fans . . . the tune that faltered would begin the next set. If the mistake was corrected, it would be business as usual—a very serious bandstand.

In addition, Jamal insisted on proper working conditions. In San Diego, we had scheduled an afternoon rehearsal, and when we got to the club, Ahmad glanced at the piano, identified it by name and year, and said, "That series was a lemon . . . you must find a better piano." They delivered another one from Los Angeles. It was still on the trailer when he played it, and it stayed there. Finally, Ahmad requested and received a Steinway.

Jamal had high standards on and off the bandstand. When an audience talked over the music, we didn't perform. Ahmad's contract rider required club management to control excessive noise. If the audience talked, we went to the nearest cinema. I remember someone threw a paper plane on the stage at Wilberforce University. That was it. We packed up our instruments and left.

When I started working with other musicians again, I observed their carelessness regarding business details. They would accept cheap hotels and sub-standard instruments, but Ahmad had a zero-tolerance policy for disrespectful treatment.

During my tenure with Ahmad, Mr. Erroll Garner asked me to join his group. He came to see us at the Tropicana in Los Angeles and told me, "Don't tell Ahmad, but I want to steal you!" Ray Brown wanted me to replace him in Oscar Peterson's trio. Ray said, "If you take this job, I can move to California." I turned down a few offers from Bill Evans as well.

ARRESTED IN SURINAME

We had some narrow escapes on the road. In June 1967, we performed in Trinidad, then, flew to Paramaribo, Suriname for our next concert. Joe Marati, a local concert promoter, met us at the airport with two unattractive women. "No, thank you," we said. After arriving at the hotel and unpacking, an announcement came over the intercom: "Will the members of the Ahmad Jamal Trio report to the dayroom!" Marati ups the ante with three beautiful women. Once again, we refused his offer.

We ate dinner and retired to our rooms early, because Ahmad wanted to test the piano in the morning. The next day, we rehearsed at the sound check and a man approached me during our rest period and asked, "How could you as a Muslim do this concert?" "What are talking about brother?" He translated the local newspaper's report, which said the concert's objective was to raise money for blood plasma and bandages for Israeli soldiers fighting in the Six-Day War. I called Ahmad over and asked the brother to re-read the article. He explained the Muslim community's anger about the concert.

Frank Gant: "I nodded off in my room and was jolted awake by the phone. The caller said, 'Mr. Gant, I am a representative of Radio Free Suriname. Please inform Ahmad Jamal, if he performs that concert, there will be dire consequences.' Shortly after I received this call, Ahmad and Jamil returned to the hotel with Mr. Marati in tow begging Jamal, "Please, perform . . . I have invested my life savings in this concert."

Marati's persuasive effort continued for three hours. Finally, Ahmad told him, "I will do this concert under two conditions: First, I will make a statement disassociating myself from the politics underlying this concert, and second I must find out who's responsible for organizing this concert." Marati accepted these stipulations, and we set out for the concert hall. Marati told the tense audience of pro-Israeli and pro-Arab groups: "There will be no concert tonight; the featured artist isn't interested in politics." One group cheered and the other jeered. We returned to the motel, and Jamil took the helm at this point, because he confronted a similar situation in Africa. The unidentified, concert promoters wanted to kill Jamil and Ahmad. And Jamil switched rooms with Ahmad and answered life-threatening phone calls throughout the night."[115]

The next morning, we developed an exit strategy for leaving the country. We told the desk clerk about our "sightseeing expedition," and head straight for the airport. The airport was empty, because one plane departed every twenty-four hours. Finally, a KLM jet arrived at 1 p.m. We lined up to board the plane and noticed a phalanx of police approaching.

The commanding officer said, "Please follow us, you aren't being arrested; however, you are being detained." They took us to an interrogation room and confiscated our luggage and passports.

"Mr. Jamal, can you pay us 8,000 dollars?"

"Mr. Gant or Mr. Nasser, can you pay us 8,000 dollars?"

As he talked, a huge fist size bug crashed against the wall. It sounded like a hand smacking the wall. I looked at Frank and Ahmad in way that told them to show no fear. Fear is a liability in a situation like this. I asked to use the phone and called the US Consulate. I made a brief statement, "The Ahmad Jamal Trio has been arrested in Suriname, please send someone to investigate." Consequently, Reuters in Georgetown, Guyana picked up the story, and the Washington Post published the following brief, "A concert promoter here said last night American jazz musician Ahmad Jamal has been arrested in neighboring Surinam. Unconfirmed reports from Surinam's capital of Paramaribo said Jamal, a convert to Islam, refused to perform in a movie theater owned by a Jew in the former Dutch colony."[116]

They transported us in separate cars to Santa Boma Prison. The officers had to stop often to cut through the thick, green foliage with their machetes. Our cells were huts with rusted, corrugated tin roofs, and a huge insect colony covered the walls. They gave us a blanket, three tin cups, and three Coke bottles: two bottles had white liquid and the other green liquid. We heard a chorus of monkeys, birds, frogs, and other strange animal sounds in the distance.

Frank said, "Ahmad, do you hear that?"

"Hear what, Frank?"

"Those crocodiles out there."

I laughed and dosed off.

A representative from the U.S. Consulate came to investigate; unfortunately, he couldn't help us.

Frank remembers, "I met a man at the hotel who claimed to be a disc jockey. Now, the same man was having sidebars with the prison warden. He said, "Mr. Gant, the food here is terrible! If you help me, alternative food arrangements can be made." I said, "We are a group so help us, not just me.""

Ahmad received a list of lawyers to contact. He selected an Asian lawyer named Lim A. Po. We could hear Mr. Po's car echoing through the jungle as he drove toward the prison. And he arrived bearing good news that an anonymous donor, sympathetic to our plight, posted bail. Free at last, we returned to the hotel and prepared to leave. We canceled our next engagement in Georgetown, Guyana, and departed Suriname having narrowly escaped a potentially life-threatening situation. When we reached American soil, Frank kissed the ground.

Back in the states, we recorded an album that projected the exact opposite of the Suriname experience—the tranquil and beautiful *Cry Young*. The Howard Roberts Chorale under the direction of the late, great pianist-composer Hale Smith delivered the goods. Ahmad's classic, funky arrangement of "Nature Boy"' was the hit single on this record. *Cry Young* found its way on the Billboard charts (No. 19 12/2/1967) at the height of the rock n' roll era without any promotional investment by Cadet. *Cry Young* was the first record that included one of my songs, a ballad entitled "Tropical Breeze." Moreover, I wrote lyrics for Jamal's composition "Minor Moods."

Another nerve-wracking experience occurred on a plane that developed mechanical problems. The flight attendants began preparing us for an emergency landing: we emptied our pockets, took off our shoes, and listened to the emergency landing instructions. The pilot circled the airport to burn fuel. A nun seated next to me prayed and in between Hail Mary's, she would scream, "Oh my God, we are going to die!" Her outbursts only intensified a stressful situation. Finally, the pilot announced the problem had been resolved and she said, "Praise God, we are going to live!" I had heard enough and said to her, "Will you shut the fuck up!"

In Newport, Kentucky, we were booked to play a weeklong engagement, but on the third night, a large, intimidating gangster came backstage with a message. The boss said, "You guys can pack up and leave." Ahmad replied, "Tell the boss, I will leave, when I am ready." I was nervous . . . these hoodlums will kill without a second thought; eventually, we left the club, and received compensation from the musician's union.

VILLAGE GATE MEMORIES

We fulfilled a long-standing engagement at the Village Gate in 1968. One night at the Gate, Babs Gonzales grabbed the microphone and said, "Jamil Nasser calls himself a Muslim now. I remember when he was George Joyner. We ate soul food together—ribs, fatback, and ham hocks. He probably still eats pork." I came off the stage, raised my fist to his face, and said, "Say one more word." I wanted to kick his ass. I said, "If you reach for that handkerchief, you're done." Babs would put black pepper in a handkerchief to blind an opponent in battle.

Moreover, I spotted the spy complicit in Oscar Dennard's murder in the audience. I started to put the bass down and confront him, but the man recognized me and slipped out.

JAMAL RECORDS

Ahmad established the Ahmad Jamal Production Corporation, Jamal Publishing, Cross Records, and Hema Music in 1969. I asked Ahmad to focus on publishing instead of a record company because I knew it was a risky venture in New York City. He took a vote, and I was outvoted. I served as the vice president of AJP Productions, Hema Music Incorporated, and the Jamal Publishing Corporation. James Snow was director of A&R for AJP and Cross Records, David Usher and Carlos Malcolm were producers, and Wesley Westbrooks was our composer.

In 1970, Ahmad Jamal Productions and Ampeg Tapes signed a distribution agreement that gave Ampeg distribution rights in the United States and Canada.[117] We recorded a broad array of artists, which included Sonny Stitt, Carlos Malcolm, Shirley Horn, Beverly Glenn, Julius Victor, Jonas Gwangwa and African Explosion, and Johnny K. The rock group, Stark Reality, recorded a children's series that featured Hoagy Carmichael.

Ahmad Jamal: Edward 'Sonny' Stitt, one of the most prominent jazz artists in the music world, has signed a three-year, exclusive recording contract with Jamal Records, it was announced by Ahmad Jamal, president of the company. "The signing of Stitt to the company," said Jamal "marks a giant step for us in building one of the finest stables of recording talent. He is indicative of the quality of recording talent that we are looking for, and we are proud to welcome him aboard." [118]

Ahmad recalls, "The masters for this recording were destroyed in a fire at the Ampeg Warehouse. A Japanese recording engineer remastered the original, and it is now available on CD. I still receive generous royalties from When Sonny Blows Blue, but I invested a substantial amount of money in Jamal Records."[119]

The New Globe and Journal printed the following review of several records produced by Jamal Productions: "Bustin Out of the Ghetto" by Carlos Malcolm and the Fireburners (AJP LPS-334) has a distinct Caribbean flavor although the sound is not confined to calypso. Who (Nubani)? by Jonas Gwangwa and African Explosion (Jamal LPS-335) is purely African with chants by the lead singer, Mamsie, and strong rhythms." Coming Again So Soon by Beverly Glenn Concert Chorale (Cross 332) is an excellent gospel album. Beverly Glenn plays the organ and leads her chorale in a concert of inspirational music. 'If I Had a Hammer' and 'The Impossible Dream' are included."[120]

In April 1970, Johnny K, a vocalist on Jamal Records, performed on *The Tonight Show,* hosted by Bill Cosby, to promote the release of his single "Come Out."[121]

The industry didn't want any more Berry Gordys. Consequently, the major record labels closed ranks against us. Our greatest challenge was distribution. For example, I delivered records to stores, yet they remained unshelved.

One day, a woman came by the office and said, "Mr. Jamal, I work for a major record company. And I just left an executive meeting this morning wherein part of the agenda involved strategies to impede your company." The company folded shortly after her warning—an expensive learning experience. Jamal Records was an artistic success and some of the records are rare collector's items.

On February 2–3, 1970, we recorded an album that continues to galvanize jazz listeners around the world, *The Awakening.* On the road, we played the music well, but in the studio, we hit a roadblock. I looked under the carpet in the studio and uncovered the problem. We were playing on a concrete surface and couldn't feel the sound vibrations. So, Ahmad asked them to build a bandstand, and we completed the recording.

June 17, 1971, we recorded two live albums at the Montreux Jazz Festival, *Outerspaceinnertime,* and *Freeflight.* These records captured the trio at a high-performance level as we explored uncharted territory. Ahmad's use of the Fender Rhodes added a different color to our sound. And the great bass with the diamond f holes I used on this date belonged to Victor Gaskins. Oliver Nelson heard our performance and told me, "I had to hire two bass players to get a sound as big as yours." He wanted me to record with him; however, Oliver expired several years after this concert.

GIG WITH MONK

Author's Note: Most books on Thelonious Monk exclude the one-week engagement Jamil played with Monk at the Aqua Lounge in Philadelphia (May 1972).

"A number of different bassists worked with the band (Monk's) after that—Dave Holland for one, Reggie Workman for another—at the Village Vanguard, the Village Gate, and the Aqua Lounge."[122]

The most recent historical tome on Monk, "Thelonious Monk; The Life and Times of an American Original" by Robin D.G. Kelley states, "Monk liked McClure[Ron] enough to keep him for him for two more gigs—a week at the Village Vanguard and two weeks at the Aqua Lounge in Philadelphia."[123] In truth, Ron McClure played one week at the Aqua Lounge, and Jamil Nasser played the other. Tenor saxophonist Paul Jeffrey recalls, "Jamil's ability to play his music without asking a lot of questions impressed Monk. Monk and Jamil had a good rapport. Monk had the utmost respect for Jamil as a person and musician."[124]

On one of our breaks, I accepted an engagement with the late, great Thelonious Monk. We met at the Baroness Nica's home, but I waited outside because of all the cats. I enjoyed the gig, everything Monk played swung, and his compositions were challenging. One night, a group of trumpet players were discussing who could play and who couldn't. Monk paced up and down just listening. Then he spun around, clapped and said, "Dizzy Gillespie respects Idrees."

Author's Note: In 1973, Ahmad signed a contract with 20th Century Fox Records—the only jazz musician signed to the label. The trio recorded "Theme from M.A.S.H." for the motion picture.

Ahmad hired Azzedin Weston, the gifted percussionist and son of Randy Weston; he heard Azzedin performing with his father in Tangier, Morocco. Randy recalls, "Ahmad Jamal came over and spent one week with me in 1970. He didn't come to play, just to visit and hang out, seeing Tangier, experiencing Morocco. I introduced him to all the people I knew, writers and so forth. That was when Ahmad first had an opportunity to hear my son Azzedin play.

Jamal really appreciated Azzedin's conga playing and actually wanted to recruit him for his band, but he didn't tell me this directly at the time. So he told our mutual friend and bassist Jamil Nasser. Jamil came back to me and said, "Hey, man, Ahmad sure likes your son, but he didn't want to ask you directly." I got excited for Azzedin and said, "Tell Ahmad to take that dude...yesterday!"[125]

These reviews offer a glimpse of this quartet:

"Pianist Ahmad Jamal and his power packed rhythm section drew standing ovations from an audience of 540 persons at Roberts Center Theatre in West Hartford. Jamal's jamming jelled perfectly from the opening number 'Swahili Land' [sic] which featured conga drummer Azzedin Weston. Weston, who is the son of pianist-composer Randy Weston, was not only strong rhythmically, but also somehow managed to get melodic sounds out of the congas like those of a string bass. Unlike many conga players, the young man played with tasteful restraint and made a substantial contribution to the group. You will probably never hear anything quite like his exciting rendition of 'Theme from M.A.S.H,' which winded through many creative crevices of sound for more than 15 minutes. Adding much along the way were Frank Gant, a quick handed and master of subtle shadings and dynamics, and Jamil S. Nasser, a bassist with a fat sound and a lithe rhythmic sense. The strong rapport among the four musicians produced a tight knit group sound in addition to the superior solo work."[126]

"Their first selection was "Theme from M.A.S.H." It was bad. This group came on cooking. They picked up their instruments and slapped you in the face with pure musical excitement. The stage was like a force field drawing you in and then taking you higher and higher on together. The bass player made his instrument cry out in joy, in pain and I could hear stories of his yesterdays, his loves and whatever for jazz forces the musician to stand naked emotionally before his audience"[127]

Baltimore journalist Bob Matthews: "The Left Bank Jazz Society concert marks one of the last sets Nasser will play with this group, since he is retiring from the music trail to go into the real estate business. 'Tis a pity, for Nasser demonstrated just how jazz bass should be played. In his hands, it became a solo instrument. He combined intricate pizzicato work with sliding glissandos, and at times provided counterpoint to the pianistics of Jamal—A truly virtuoso performance."[128]

Rappers and rap groups such as Jay Z, Ice-T, De La Soul, Nas, KRS-One, and Young Jeezy sampled six albums: Jamal Plays Jamal, Freeflight, Poinciana Revisited, The Awakening, Tranquility, and Outerspaceinnertime.

I left Jamal's ensemble to pursue a real estate career in 1976. In addition, I wanted to make my mark as a leader. I gave three years notice prior to leaving, because we developed such a strong rapport over the years. I recorded eighteen albums with him between 1964 and 2000.

8

REAL ESTATE AND MUSIC

For these three weeks Gibbs [Terry] has the outstanding backing of pianist Walter Bishop, Jr., bassist Jamil Nasser and Ray Mosca on drums. They hit the ground swinging Monday night and if past experience with Gibbs is any index, it'll stay that way.

–RICHARD M. SUDHALTER

In 1972, I worked as a part-time broker at George T. Smith Real Estate in Westbury, Long Island; four years later, I decided to sell real estate full-time and perform on a part-time basis. By this time, road fatigue, family obligations, and my desire for financial advancement prompted my exit from Jamal's trio. My friend, Charlie Johnson, had established an economic foothold in real estate and convinced me to do likewise. From our office located in New Rochelle, I sold houses throughout Westchester County. One of my clients was F.O.I. Captain, Yusef Shah, who served under Malcolm X and Louis Farrakhan at Mosque Number Seven in Harlem. He told me after Elijah Muhammad passed his son Wallace paid the old guard to leave.

131

Charlie owned several apartment buildings in Harlem, and he deputized me to collect cash rental fees. One afternoon, after a collection run, I confronted thugs sitting on my car. I flipped back my jacket as if I had a gun and said, "Can I help you motherfuckers?" They backed off, and I drove off as my hands shook violently on the steering wheel. Zaid Nasser, son and alto saxophonist recalls, "I waited in the car as Dad collected rent. I heard the door swing open and saw a huge man with a pipe chasing Dad. Dad took a bat out of the car . . . whacked him across the head, and we took off."

In New Rochelle, someone broke into my apartment and stole my Rubner bass. I spent months asking bassists all over New York City to uncover their instruments. Eventually, I found the bass at a pawnshop in New Rochelle. I called the police, identified a mark on it, and brought my baby home. Unfortunately, a few years later, I loaned out the bass for a Bryant Park concert series and someone walked off with it again.

Working with Al Haig

In 1976, Al Haig and I formed a fruitful musical partnership, which blossomed during our regular gig at Gregory's: *"It appears that Al Haig has found a home base at Gregory's, an intimate music room and bar on 63rd Street and First Avenue. He appears there Monday and Tuesday evenings along with bassist Jamil Nasser and guitarist Chuck Wayne. Nasser, who spent 12 years as Ahmad Jamal's regular bassist, claims he only plays now 'as a hobby.' Hobby or not his solos are impressive."*[129]

Al told me about how Charlie Parker and Dizzy Gillespie auditioned him: "They came into the Spotlite on 52nd Street silently took out their horns and jumped on the bandstand. Then Bird told the other musicians except Haig to clear the stage. After playing four tunes with Al, Bird and Diz said, 'You're our piano player . . . let's go!' They took him from the Spotlite to where they were working. Parker and Gillespie's endorsement represents real credentials, not record company, industry, or nightclub credentials bestowed by non-musicians. And this association alone should have advanced Haig's career. By the way, Hank Jones said, "Al Haig taught us how to comp behind a soloist. We couldn't learn that from Bud Powell."

I loved working with Al. He had a great touch, colorful chord voicings, and could swing. We recorded ten albums. In 1978, we toured England, and it bothered Al that I never had my own record date (in the US), so he asked me to choose the songs and concept. So, I thought of a train transporting Duke's music around the world so each track begins with locomotive effects from my bass. I played the melodies on "Body and Soul" and "I Let a Song Go Out of My Heart." Al fought with Spotlite Record executives to include me as a co-leader on *Expressly Ellington*. Furthermore, he told me, some booking agents asked him to hire another bass player, but he refused and stood up for me.

When we played at a London jazz club, I saw a two-hundred and fifty old year-old bass sitting in the corner and bought it from the club owner. Sam Kolstein, the master bass technician, overhauled it. My life-long search was over—this was the one. She survived a car wreck and provided a buffer between Eddie Heywood and the floor at Jimmy Weston's. In both cases, the bass needed extensive repair work.

On November 16, 1982, Al Haig died of a sudden heart attack; unfortunately, he had only three hundred dollars in the bank. Cobi Narita, Art D'Lugoff, and I produced a piano summit entitled "A Pianorama Valentine for Al Haig"—an afternoon of music presented by the piano trios of Monty Alexander, Harold Mabern, Cedar Walton, Barry Harris, Dick Katz, and Walter Bishop Jr. Ahmad Jamal canceled due to inclement weather. All the proceeds went to the Haig family.

WORKING WITH CYBILL SHEPHERD

Actress and vocalist, Cybill Shepherd: The Memphis "Vanilla" connection came about through her brother, Bill Shepherd. "He produced the first 'Beale

Street Blues Festival[Video],' with B.B. King and all kinds of incredible people, made a film of it, and ran the videotape of it when he visited me in California. He said, 'What are you doing making records with people like Stan Getz? You can't imagine how great the musicians are in Memphis.'" *Watching the videotape, Cybill Shepherd was reminded of the blues and jazz associations of her home town. "I saw Phineas and his bassist Jamil Nasser, and this great saxophonist and arranger, Fred Ford. I knew at once I had to get back home if I wanted to make a record I'd be satisfied with."[130]*

I established a working relationship with Cybill Shepherd in 1978. Cybill, a fellow Memphian, wanted to develop her skills as a jazz vocalist. She possessed a pleasant voice and hired me as her bassist and East Coast musical director. We recorded *Vanilla* with a cast of great Memphis musicians, which included Phineas Newborn on piano. Prior to the session, I asked Fred Ford to arrange the music, but when we got to the studio, he pulled out some corny, stock arrangements. I said, "Fred, these are high school combo arrangements." And he had to rearrange the music. Meanwhile, I took Cybill to meet my parents, enjoy their down-home cuisine, and discuss plans for furthering her jazz career.

She made her New York debut at Reno Sweeney. We had a good rehearsal on the afternoon of the gig. I arrived early and found Cybill talking with friends. She introduced me and asked if they could sing with us. I said, "Cybill, let me hear them first." They were horrible! I told her, "Either they go or I go. I am a professional and as such will not perform with amateurs. Moreover, New York critics will pan your performance without pity or mercy." She trusted my judgment and withdrew her request, but this engagement marked the end of our association. A position on our bandstand must be earned and respected.

The following review in the *New York Times* justified my concerns:

"Cybill Shepherd, who has been a successful model, a not-so-successful film actress, and a less successful cabaret singer, is back in town in the guise of a jazz singer. At Reno Sweeney, where she is appearing through tomorrow night, she is backed by the Memphis All-Stars, a trio that includes a

strong and capable jazz pianist, Harold Mabern, as well as Jamil Nasser, a bassist who played for many years with the pianist Ahmad Jamal, and a gray-bearded saxophonist, Fred Ford, who ranges from a deep, breathy, Hawkins-like approach to occasional gentle squeals. It is these musicians who give Miss Shepherd's performance what jazz qualities it has."[131]

WORKING WITH THE LOUIS HAYES QUARTET

"Mr. Hayes's reputation as a seasoned drummer whose maturity exceeded his years spread throughout New York, and before long he was among the most sought-after drummers in New York. Since then he has formed and co-led a number of successful groups. His current quartet—Harold Mabern, piano; Jamil Nasser (formerly with the Ahmad Jamal Trio), bass; and Frank Strozier, alto—has the potential to be the most dynamic group of 1979. "All of the guys in the group have known each other for years," Mr. Hayes said from New York. "Frank Strozier did a record with Woody (Shaw) awhile back, and Woody and I both agreed that if I was going to start a group, Frank would be an excellent choice to begin with. Frank and Harold (Mabern) have been friends for years (both men are from Tennessee) so that's how I got my pianist. Bassist Jamil Nasser is the newest member of the group. He joined earlier this year, replacing Stafford James. Each of us in the group has been thinking in terms of this type of music, we've just now come together."[132]

When I joined the Louis Hayes Quartet, I looked forward to working regularly with Lou and the great alto saxophonist and composer Frank Strozier. Unfortunately, ten years later, Frank's frustration with the music business and the inadequacy of saxophone reeds compelled him to teach and play piano for his own enjoyment—a tremendous loss to the jazz community.

Journalist, Owen McNally: "Right from the opening number, Hayes and his three colleagues began at a very high voltage level with their all-acoustic, neo-bop brand of electrifying jazz. Much of the surging musical current was sparked by alto saxophonist and flutist Frank Strozier. Strozier opened the night on the dizzying sort of energy peak that most saxophonists dare not try to scale in a whole night's, a week's, or even a month's work. Although small in stature, Strozier is a saxophone colossus."[133]

In August, we performed in Holland, Germany, Belgium, Denmark, and Switzerland. In East Germany, Louis had an argument with a flight attendant; she closed the plane door with me on one side—the band on the other. It was a miss the plane, miss the concert scenario, so I used a local pianist and drummer on some selections and played solo bass as well. Moreover, Babs Gonzales performed a few numbers with me: Babs passed away about six months later, and I was glad we parted company on good terms. After receiving a standing ovation and full payment, I paid Frank, Harold, and Louis.

Our tour ended at the Willisau Festival (Switzerland) with two special guests, Freddie Hubbard and the great vocalist Leon Thomas. We played Strozier's arrangement of Marvin Gaye's "What's Going On." In 1979, Hubbard reigned supreme on trumpet, an exciting soloist who always pushed the envelope. Some trumpet players are very safety conscious, but Freddie could switch gears at any time— he can play a beautiful ballad—then jump on the racehorse.

I wanted the promoter to pay us before the concert, so I went looking for him and the band started without me. Freddie said, "Where is the bass player?" I canceled my brief protest and played. Promoters in Europe are notorious for absconding with the money while the musicians are on stage. Similarly, notorious were the propositions I received to smuggle drugs inside my bass. The recruiters must have noticed that I wasn't searched or detained. In those days, I could buy a children's ticket for the bass. The offers were lucrative, but I turned them down.

THE HAROLD MABERN TRIO

Harold and I had a three-week duo engagement at the Village Gate, and we attempted to play all the songs we knew but never came close. Our trio included drummers like Walter Bolden, Frank Gant, Walter Perkins, and Idris Muhammad. In addition, we supported George Coleman, Eddie "Cleanhead" Vinson, Budd Johnson, Buddy Tate, Tom Harrell, Harold Vick, and many others.

Author's Note: The following superlative reviews reflect the special musical relationship between Harold Mabern and Jamil Nasser:

"Harrell's phrasing had a well-honed cutting edge that gave an extra poignant quality to his expressiveness. He was given solid support by a trio consisting of pianist Harold Mabern, bassist Jamil Nasser, and the drummer and leader Walter Bolden."[134]

"Mr. Mabern concentrates on just the essence of his swinging drive when he is cut loose to solo on an up-tempo piece. When the trio is playing behind Mr. Vinson's saxophone, it is a crisp, energizing group firmly driven by Mr. [Curtis] Boyd's drums and soaring on Mr. Nasser's insistent use of the upper register."[135]

"[Harold] Ashby was backed by a genuine working trio, not just a makeshift pickup band of musicians who never worked together before. Led by drummer Walter Bolden, the trio also consisted of pianist Harold Mabern and bassist Jamil Nasser. While Ashby took a break now and then, the trio would serve a hot, zesty sampler of its own kind of jazz cooking. Mabern is an empathetic accompanist as well as a strong soloist who gets a rich sound from the piano with his full-bodied chordal passages. Nasser, who worked in the Ahmad Jamal Trio for 11 years, turned every one of his solos into pleasant individual pieces that sparkled with thematic variations and witty allusions to other tunes. Bolden's drumming had an extra snap to it as he seemed especially happy to be home again in Hartford, leading a first-rate trio backing Ashby, a tenor who embodies the very best in the classic big band tradition."[136]

George Coleman, Harold Mabern, Frank Strozier, and I grew up in Memphis together and played all over the world, but one city never extended an invitation: our hometown Memphis.

9

STRANGERS IN OUR HOMETOWN

Memphis does not know what we accomplished, where we've been, or how we got there.

–JAMIL NASSER

MEMPHIS MUSICIANS

In 1990, I watched a documentary entitled, *All Day and All Night: Memories from Beale Street Musicians,* which featured interviews with Fred Ford, Andrew "Sunbeam" Mitchell, Honeymoon Garner, and Robert Talley. And they failed to mention Jimmie Lunceford, Phineas Newborn Jr., Harold Mabern, Booker Little, Frank Strozier, or me. Harold and George happen to be watching, and they were as incensed as I was. So, we decided to boycott Memphis. Our musical progenitors like Memphis Minnie, Jimmie Lunceford, W.C. Handy, Otto Lee, and many others created a great musical environment for us. In the late '40s and early '50s, many great musicians like Count Basie, Duke Ellington, John Coltrane, and Benny Bailey performed in Memphis.

We lived on opposite ends of the city: Booker T. Washington High School was in South Memphis, and Manassas High School was in North Memphis. The Booker Teasers included Phineas

Newborn, Floyd Newman, Calvin Newborn, Charles Crosby, Louis Smith, and me. The Manassas Rhythm Bombers included its bandleader, trumpeter Matthew Garrett (Dee Dee Bridgewater's father), George Coleman, Frank Strozier, Hank Crawford, Charles Lloyd, Harold Mabern, Booker Little, and Evans Bradshaw. We would often jam together, which culminated in the fusion of Memphis style blues with bebop. Because on gigs we had to interpolate jazz tunes into the blues songs.

We eventually left Memphis; one group migrated to Chicago, and the other to New York City. George Coleman, Booker Little, Frank Strozier, and Harold Mabern went to Chicago. Phineas Newborn, Calvin Newborn, Louis Smith, and I went directly to New York. We joined the top ranks of the jazz world, and the rich musical environment in Memphis prepared us. Most of us avoided alcohol and drug addiction. And we hired each other for gigs, record dates, and workshops.

Edward Louis Smith and Booker Little were two of our great jazz trumpeters. In fact, Smith gave his cousin Booker trumpet lessons. Edward Louis Smith developed a style like Clifford Brown. Louis, like, Clifford, loved Fats Navarro; however, Smith had a legato approach to articulation, whereas Clifford played staccato. Louis came to New York, a couple years after me. The vagaries of a jazz musician's life, however, which included missing meals and empty pockets, didn't suit his personality, so I encouraged him to leave. When Louis worked with Horace Silver, he asked him to comp at a softer dynamic level. And Silver said, "Well, I guess that's it," and fired him. Smith left New York and took a teaching position at a high school in Atlanta. Eventually, he became a tenured jazz professor at the University of Michigan for twenty years. In 1978, Louis, George Coleman, Harold Mabern, and I reunited to record "Just Friends." Louis played an excellent solo on "Oleo."

Author's Note: Trumpeter Freddie Hubbard reflecting upon Booker's influence said: "Booker was one of the fastest trumpeters I ever heard. I used to come to Chicago every Sunday to play, when I lived in Indianapolis. At a place called the Rendezvous, where Bunky Green and Frank Strozier worked. It was a slick place; the bandstand used to revolve. Frank Strozier and Booker Little would run me off, because they played fast. They tried to see how fast they could play."[137]

"We ended up working around town in Slide Hampton's Octet. Every night it was good to go to work because there was going to be a challenge. We'd try to kick each other's behind, but we liked each other."[138] *Freddie wrote a beautiful ballad, "Lament for Booker" in tribute to his fallen comrade.*

John Coltrane gave George Coleman his horn, so Miles could hear him play, which turned out to be a quasi-audition. And, in 1963, George became a member of the Miles Davis Quintet. Miles respected Coleman's musicianship and harbored curiosity about the environment that produced him:

"Before I left New York, I had had tryouts for the band and that's where I got all those Memphis musicians—Coleman, Strozier, and Mabern. (They had gone to school with the great young trumpet player Booker Little, who soon after this died of leukemia, and the pianist Phineas Newborn. I wonder what they were doing down there when all the guys came through that same school)."[139]

Harold Mabern, a brilliant pianist, composer, and educator who performed with Lee Morgan, Betty Carter, Freddie Hubbard, Wes Montgomery, and many others. He recorded classic albums as a leader like "Greasy Kids Stuff" and "Rakin and Scrapin."

Frank Strozier is a master alto saxophonist and flutist who developed a unique approach to both instruments. In 1960, Sid Lazard observed, "Strozier is a triple threat. In addition to being an alto saxophonist of the highest quality, he is also a gifted writer and arranger. The guy is just plain great—one of the freshest, swinginest, just all around bestest musicians on the jazz scene."[140]

Tenor saxophonist Charles Lloyd, in addition to playing with Cannonball Adderley and Chico Hamilton, led his popular quartet from 1966 to 1968. His 1967 album Forest Flower sold over one million copies. Lloyd exposed jazz to the rock 'n' roll audience by playing venues like the Fillmore East.

Hank Crawford, the great alto saxophonist and arranger for Ray Charles, played an important role in the development of the "smooth jazz" saxophone concept.

Charles Crosby and Evans Bradshaw are two Memphis musicians seldom mentioned in jazz literature. "Charles Crosby, a legendary drummer, was born in Memphis on November 26, 1931. Charles entered the music profession at 16 years old—a year after his first lessons. He gigged with B.B. King's road band in the early '50s. After leaving Memphis, Crosby led his own group in Columbus, Ohio. He migrated to New York City in 1958. Charles performed and recorded with Jimmy Smith, Rashaan Roland Kirk, Rusty Bryant, and Joe Alexander.

Charles wasn't answering his phone and missing gigs, so I went to his apartment. I asked the manager to open his door, and we found his body. He had contracted ptomaine poisoning from a can of pork and beans. I found and kept his passport.

Ben Branch, tenor saxophonist and bandleader, who led bands that supported Martin Luther King and Jesse Jackson, shared his reflections on Dr. Kings last moments: "After a staff meeting, as Branch was walking down the motel stairs, Dr. King ran out to the porch and yelled, 'Ben, please don't forget to play "Precious Lord" for me tonight. I want you to play it like you never played it before.' Before King could say another word, Branch could hear the shot ringing. "Dr. King wanted to see all black musicians come together and promote the musical culture of blacks," said Branch.[141]

In 1972, Isaac Hayes became the first African American to receive an Oscar for the *Shaft* soundtrack. Al Green, Booker T and the MGs, Willie Mitchell, Rufus and Carla Thomas, and the Memphis Horns injected the favor of Memphis into rhythm and blues. Chris Woods was a great alto saxophonist who worked with Dizzy Gillespie, Clark Terry, Buddy Rich, and Sy Oliver. Maurice White, the drummer and leader of Earth, Wind, and Fire was raised in Memphis and graduated from Booker T. Washington High School. We were proud of the younger Memphis musicians who came after us like James Williams, Mulgrew Miller, Donald Brown, Tony Reedus, and Bill Mobley. They did their homework and asked many questions. In 1992, we recorded *The Memphis Convention*. But some of us had previously convened on Beale Street in 1977.

10

First Beale Street Music Festival

"*Despite years of planning and discussion of developing Memphis as a tourist destination and rebuilding a downtown entertainment center around the Beale Street Historic District, city leaders did not fully grasp the cultural significance of Elvis or the lasting appeal of any of the city's musical legends and landmarks. Not only did the local leaders fail to recognize the global impact of Memphis music and those who created it, but they did not understand the significance of the city of Memphis itself, as a place.*" [142] "*With bulldozers and wrecking cranes for pallbearers, the famous street is being put to the ground. The saddest part, however, is that Beale Street, which for many years cut a mighty fine strut through downtown, is going out quietly.*" [143]*

"*On a hot sunny afternoon, soon after I arrived in Memphis, a few of us freshmen decided it was time to see the world-famous Beale Street. We arrived too late; Beale Street had been razed. Where there had once been shops, bars, cafes, funeral homes, dry cleaners, barbershops, churches, professional offices, music halls, and other businesses, there were empty, boarded up buildings, and vacant, litter-strewn lots. We later learned that those white people in charge, in the governments of Memphis and Washington D.C., had purposely destroyed Beale Street, using as their cover urban renewal.*" [144]

"But ask many people how Memphis in May got its start, and they won't be able to tell you. They assume, as do most of us, that the city's largest festival just sprang into existence, with thousands of people crowding Tom Lee Park for the Sunset Symphony, and hundreds of teams hauling giant cookers downtown for the World Championship Barbeque Cooking Contest—just two events in a May calendar packed with a month full of activities. "You have to remember that Memphis was in a depression back then, and the city had no money to do anything," says developer Lyman Aldrich, the first president of Memphis in May, and Chairman Emeritus of the organization.

"I was in line to be the president in 1977, so I told them I was taking it away from the chamber. I wanted to bring in more young people, men and women, black and white, who were willing to turn our city around. Memphis in May was huge in trying to create jobs and bring more people downtown," says Aldrich. "The first year introduced the Sunset Symphony and the Beale Street Music Festival, both events a success. I thought if we can work around the international (component) to create some economic activity from around the world for investing in Memphis and create some events locally, then we could create jobs for hotels, motels, and bars and so forth, and if we were really lucky, we could get businesses from a foreign country to come here and create jobs."[145]

About 70 percent of the visitors at the 2009 Beale Street Music Festival were from outside of Memphis and provided $23 million in direct business revenue, and another 23.2 million in indirect sales, all of which supported 577 jobs earning more than $14 million. The festival honors a different foreign country every year—Japan in 1977."[146]

Robert Palmer revealed the true origin of the Beale Street Music Festival in the New York Times: The Memphis In May Festival began in 1977, when two Memphis jazz musicians, saxophonist Fred Ford and bassist Jamil Nasser, began talking about how much they would like to see some of their old friends again. "We were listening to some of those old Jazz at the Philharmonic Concert albums," Mr. Ford recalled last week at the 1982 Beale Street Festival. "We talked about bringing all the jazz giants from Memphis back here to play together to do some concerts and onstage jam *sessions like Jazz at the Philharmonic. A lawyer down here, Irvin Salky, put his money $30,000 [$75,000] on the line that is how we put the first of these festivals together."[147]*

In Japan and Europe, I encountered many people who knew the significance of our history, but Memphis never acknowledged us. And I wanted to investigate why. So, prior to coming to Memphis, I asked Perry Allen, a local music programmer, to schedule a meeting with the Memphis area Chamber of Commerce. Two weeks later, he told me everything was in order, so Nathan Woodard and I flew to Memphis. But when we called to confirm our appointment, they had no record of it. I asked Perry, "Why did you have us fly here for nothing?" I was livid. Then I called Estelle Axton, co-owner of Stax Records, and she got us on the schedule. On November 26, 1973, we gave them a historical outline of our Memphis blues and jazz legacy and a music festival proposal. They were shocked, and said, "We must have this . . . it would be a great financial and social boost for the city." Yet they couldn't find sponsors.

In 1977, we showcased great Memphis musicians, who graciously waived their normal fees, at the first Beale Street Music Festival. I started my booking agency, Jayeed Festivals, to manage the business logistics. As the musical director and the only bassist for the jazz segment, I played for ten hours with brief breaks during the re-staging process. The musicians received limousine service from the airport and advance payment. I called upon the organizational skills of Cobi Narita and Irvin Salky to assist in planning the festival.

Attorney and sponsor of the inaugural Beale Street Music Festival, Irvin Salky: "My father owned a pawnshop on Beale Street, the cultural nucleus of Memphis, which featured great local artists, traveling bands, and musicians. In the seventies, Schwab's was the only store open on Beale Street. I couldn't stand by and watch such a historical street fall into disrepair. I wanted to play a role in restoring Beale Street and honoring great Memphis musicians, because the city didn't recognize or respect them.

The Memphis in May Committee asked me to consider merging the music festival with their barbeque contest. My friend, the late Jerry Fanion, who worked for the Shelby County Community Service Division, saxophonist Fred Ford, and bassist Jamil Nasser, formed the core committee who organized the first Beale Street Music Festival. Fred organized the gospel and blues musicians within the Memphis area, and Jamil assembled the expatriate musicians located in New York and elsewhere. We planned the festival in six weeks.

On his last visit, Sonny Criss had a horrible encounter with the Memphis police and vowed never to return to the city. It took four weeks to persuade him to make his last appearance in Memphis; Sonny expired on November 19, 1977.

The festival facilitated Beale Street's redevelopment process, but the current festival could be anywhere, because many of the artists aren't Memphians. The Memphis musicians gave the festival its unique flavor. I gave each artist a plaque as a token of my appreciation and provided financial assistance as well."[148]

The legendary Nate D. Williams emceed the festival and wrote the following introduction: "Memphis has taken the lead in bringing about a merger of the past, present and future on a grand scale. This two-day festival will be a musical feast for music lovers and historians all over the world. The Beale Street Festival will feature living legends right in the center of the famous street that nurtured their musical talents.

Beale Street had a conversation for anyone who was fortunate enough to be on or around it. The powerful pulses and rhythms of Memphis gospel, blues, and jazz resonated around the world. Simultaneously, Memphis and New Orleans were musical toss-a-coin choices, and New Orleans won the toss in terms of receiving more publicity. This homecoming of living legends from Memphis has never happened before.

We heard the soulful moans of Bessie Smith and Ma Rainey; the mellow wail of Buster Bailey's clarinet. The classic riffs of the Jimmie Lunceford Band propelled by the intense rhythm and beat of Jimmie Crawford's drums; the sights and sounds of Booker Washington's pit band drummers at the Palace Theatre, driving the chorus line into a high-kicking frenzy.

We saw W.C. Handy sitting on the wooden crate converting all the sights and sounds into manuscript. The sharecroppers and laborers dancing the jig 'till the early dawn and the aromas of fried pork chops, turnip greens, and black-eyed peas . . . That was Beale Street!"

The performers included Phineas Newborn, George Coleman, Calvin Newborn, Sonny Criss, Edward Louis Smith, Calvin Jones, Dick Griffin, Frank Strozier, Harold Mabern, Nathan Woodard, B.B. King, Furry Lewis, Fred Ford, Al Green (scheduled but didn't perform), Mickey Tucker, and Rufus Thomas.

Our families, classmates, and teachers came out to hear us. Some remembered our early jam sessions and gigs. The love and support we received was heartfelt.

In December 1978, I along with Cybill Shepherd, Phineas Newborn Jr., Memphis Slim, Fred Ford, and The Beale Street Orchestra participated in a fundraiser to restore the Orpheum Theatre: *The Memphis Development Corporation purchased the Orpheum in 1977. "It was billed as the "50th Birthday Gala." said, Miss V. Rutledge Forney, executive producer of the show, along with Orpheum project director Hillsman L. Wright, and an official of the Memphis Development Foundation, which sponsored the show and was planning the renovation of the theater said, "Income from 100 dollar-a-seat ticket's is expected to net in the rough neighborhood of 220,000 dollars once expenses are deducted. The foundation rescued this historic theater from the destruction wrought by urban renewal (removal)."[149]*

Robert Palmer reviewed the 1982 festival: "Coleman, Strozier, and Mabern played for ecstatic festival audiences on Saturday and Sunday nights and in the early morning hours of Sunday morning at Club Paradise. It was difficult to imagine anyone playing with more fire, feeling, and technical expertise than Coleman displayed in Memphis. Mabern playing the grand piano with such force that it rocked back and forth on stage, and Strozier unleashing torrential solos while looking unflappably bemused, were playing at the same impressive level."[150]

My dream to play Memphis at least once a year remained as such. And the current Beale Street Music Festival is more of a pop festival than a jazz and blues one. When I walked down Beale Street, in 1990, tears came to my eyes. What happen to our street? And the mediocre bands in the mostly empty nightclubs kept me on the sidewalk. The proper restoration of Beale Street could have positioned Memphis to rival New Orleans as a tourist destination. But the current Beale Street doesn't bear a faint resemblance to the original because the planning committee didn't consult the old-timers. It's a dismal failure from a cultural standpoint, like a can of plastic worms. And Elvis Presley's statue is an insult. He had nothing to do with Beale Street, except as a listener. When I played music on Beale Street, we had iceboxes. And Elvis not only delivered ice to the Mitchell Hotel but would hang around to watch Calvin Newborn's performance antics, which included his controversial hip wiggles. Where are the statues of Jimmie Lunceford and Phineas Newborn Jr. on Beale Street? We are still strangers in our hometown.

11

REUNIONS

For an ad hoc group pulled together quickly for this engagement, there was an unusual sense of unity in the trio, particularly between Mr. Weston and Mr. Nasser, an agile bassist who did not simply accompany Mr. Weston and take an occasional solo but was an involved force in some of Mr. Weston's provocative and unusual developments.

—JOHN S. WILSON

Jamil was my favorite bass player.

—RANDY WESTON

RANDY WESTON

Randy is one of the few bandleaders I never refuse a date with. Anytime he calls. If I have something I can cancel, it's not a matter of how much (money) because Randy is a musician's king, and you give kings consideration. You see, Randy should have monuments built to him already. So, I think that it's one of the greatest things that ever happen that the true link between Monk and

Ellington would be doing these tributes' (portrait album series) 'cause nobody is more qualified to do them than Randy Weston. Randy is not only a super performer, a super pianist, he's also a super writer. We, artists, didn't need critics to tell us that. We've known for years! We exchange knowledge. We don't criticize.[151]

In July 1981, I accompanied Randy Weston in a historic concert with the Boston Pops Symphony Orchestra conducted by John Williams. We performed Melba Liston's arrangement of Randy's composition, "Three African Queens." In addition, the late, great composer and pianist Hale Smith masterfully orchestrated each selection. Despite not seeing the music until the sound check, we nailed it. Idrees Sulieman's big, beautiful sound floored the trumpet section because puffed cheeks are taboo in the classical trumpet world, yet Idrees played great with them.

Boston Globe review: "*The first movement, 'Royal Lady,' honors according to Weston those who sweep floors, tend families, and work with dignity. It danced floatingly on a waltz signature, which Weston alternately spiced with dashes of funk and dense lines. After Nasser's melodic solo and four bar swaps between piano and drums, Big Black delivered a cannonade from his African drums. Part two, 'Portrait of Billie Holiday,' opened with a lacy, introspective piano cadenza yielding to Sulieman's blowing sustained single notes in a bluesy interlude which the orchestra eventually fleshed out into a palette of soft colors. The third movement was 'Blues for Elma Lewis.' Weston opened with a dynamic introduction, followed by a vamp from Gant's hi-hat symbol which materialized into a statement from the trombone and trumpet section. This movement contained an impressive bass solo featuring some speedy downward fingering and Weston's thick chord voicings with flashes of dissonances.*"[152]

In the same year, we played the Spoleto Festival in South Carolina with an all-star group: Idrees Sulieman on trumpet, James Spaulding on alto sax, Bill Saxton on tenor sax, Randy Weston on piano, Ed Blackwell on drums, me on bass, and Big Black on tumbas. We performed a suite commissioned by the festival called "The Africans."

Randy Weston: "Jamil possessed an entrepreneurial spirit and insisted upon proper compensation. Sometimes, I couldn't afford him . . . had to argue like crazy with Jean-Philippe Allard to pay his fee. In 1989, we recorded the three-album portrait series in Paris, and Jamil negotiated a higher fee than I received as the leader."[153]

Concerning this session Kapchan wrote: "Though Portrait of Thelonious Monk is a tribute to one of the world's most revered composer/pianists, Weston does not imitate Monk with musicians Idris Muhammad, Jamil Nasser, bassist, and Eric Asante, percussionist. Randy plays some of Monk's compositions, Weston style. He combines the sounds and rhythms that he has gathered in his 30 years as a musician, with the New Orleans sound of Idris Muhammad, a touch of Africa from Asante, and the deep bluesy Memphis sound of Jamil Nasser. Together in Ferber Studios in Paris, they produced a bit of magic, all in a single day and with no prior rehearsal, no music sheets, just sheer joy."[154]

Author's Note: Randy Weston, a phenomenal pianist and composer, whose conceptual approach rests on a foundation of African rhythms as well as the pianistic stylings of Duke Ellington and Thelonious Monk. Mr. Weston is a warm and friendly human being. For example, I was two hours late for my interview, but instead of cursing me out—he was patience and understanding. Randy articulated the cultural importance of Africa when an abysmal ignorance prevailed about its glorious history.

In February 1990, at the Village Vanguard, Weston floored an audience with a kinetic, musical gesture. The last tune faded to a whisper, and the audience screamed. Startled, I jumped up to see what happened . . . I missed it. "Randy can really show off when he wants to," my father said as he left the bandstand. Randy laughed and strolled pass the audience.

Over the last thirty years, I have heard Randy in many different settings. For example, I remember a duo engagement with Randy and my father at an art gallery in the East Village, where a homeless, drunk stumbled up near the piano. Mr. Weston gave him about sixty seconds to do his dance number, but the brother got too comfortable. Randy stood up, continued to play with his right hand, waved his left hand, and said firmly, "All right baby, that's enough!" The man quickly cleared the area.

151

Red was a Texas swinger, a real blues player. I played Red's last recorded live gig. We went to Japan with Lou Donaldson on alto and Jamil Nasser on bass. Jamil had to go get him at his house in Texas to bring him to the airport. It took about a half hour for Red to walk through the airport to get to the gate. He was in such bad shape for the first two or three days. –Jimmy Cobb

Red told me that he asked John Coltrane if he preferred playing avant-garde as opposed to standards and straight-ahead jazz. And Coltrane said, "I love playing the standards, but I can't go back." – Jamil Nasser

RED GARLAND

Author's Note: In 1965, Red Garland left the New York jazz scene, his mother passed that year, and he decided to remain in Dallas. A feature article in the Texas Monthly paints a picture of Red's career in 1977:

"There were a few trips for club appearances in Los Angeles and New York and there was a recording session for a German label. But for the international jazz constituency he acquired during and after his four years with Davis, Garland has been among the missing. There were rumors that he was dead, ill, retired, drying out, despondent or working for the post office. In 1975, Red dropped out altogether. When Red returned to the keyboard, he made a painful discovery. 'After laying off for a year and a half, I was out of shape.' When famed R&B singer and fellow Texan Johnny Taylor asked Red to tour with him, he replied, 'I would rather wash dishes than play that type of music.' He began making public appearances again in 1976."[155]

Red's long absence created a demand among his fans to hear him. I met Takao Ishizuka, a Japanese promoter, who asked if I could bring him to Japan. So, I contacted Red and he agreed to perform. Our departure was set for January 16, 1980. We were booked to play fifteen concerts over a three-week period. And everyone was ready, except Red. I called Dallas to check his status. When Red answered the phone, he said, "Man, I don't feel like going . . . reschedule the dates for another time." "You signed the contract and they're expecting us. Lou Donaldson and Jimmy Cobb are en route. Red, I'm coming to get you, too late to back out."

I flew to Dallas and took a cab to his house. I greeted Red's wife, Lilly, and she pointed to his room. As soon as I entered, Red said, "Can we leave tomorrow?"

"No, we're leaving today."

I grabbed his leg and pulled him halfway out of the bed.

He yelled, "God dammit, you gonna make me go?"

"Yes!" I yelled back.

I asked Lilly for his clothes; she pointed to a pile of clothes, all plaid, from the socks to the hat. I packed his bag, and we took a cab to the airport. We arrived as the plane was boarding. Red took two-steps a minute and complained every step of the way.

"Man, I need a damn beer . . . why do we have to go now?"

"Red, they have beer on the plane." I called the gate, asked them to hold the plane, requested a wheelchair, and pushed him as fast as I could. We boarded the plane and took off.

The next evening, we played the first song, and Red had some trouble. So, he looked at Lou, who sounded great; then he looked at me. Finally, he looked at Jimmy and continued to stare. I called them together for a meeting.

Red told Jimmy, "I just need to hear tinty-boom, tinty-boom."

Jimmy said, "Don't tell me how to play, go to hell," and stormed out.

The record company wanted to record immediately, but I advised them to wait. Red needed time to get his chops together.

One of his Japanese fans invited us to his home to see a room covered with all of Red's albums. Red seemed surprised by the sheer volume of his catalogue.

Alto saxophonist, Lou Donaldson: "Jamil wanted to establish a long-term business relationship with Takao Ishizuka, so he asked us to keep Japanese women out of our hotel rooms, but Red ignored his request. He encountered many problems managing Red on this tour."[156]

Our next gig was on a Japanese island, where a plane departed every other day. After the gig, Red stayed up all night drinking beer. The plane departed at five o'clock the next morning, so I told him, "Don't go to sleep; we must catch that plane." I knocked on his door a few hours later—no answer. I had the housekeeper open his door. Red said, 'Man, I'm not going anywhere; I will meet you at the next gig.'

By this time, I was at my wits end dealing with this madness. I told him, "I can see you're not happy, so I am going pay you and send you home." I said this knowing that he didn't want to forfeit this lucrative tour. Red told me 750 dollars a week was the maximum salary he received from Miles Davis. I secured a $ 5,000 advance for each of us.

He asked me, "You think you know me, don't you?"

He knew I was calling his bluff.

Red pulled himself together and started to play his ass off. I breathed a sigh of relief. We sold out every performance and received standing ovations from our Japanese fans. Moreover, we recorded the last two live concerts on the album *Fine and Dandy* and made a studio album of pretty ballads entitled, *In the Wee Small Hours.*

Takao wanted the same group for a return engagement in July 1982. I wrote him the following disclaimer, "Red was supposed to appear here in New York on February 2-7, 1982, but canceled on short notice. His wife called me on the morning he was to leave Dallas and told me Red was fearful about the inclement weather." So, I hired Milt Jackson to replace him.

"Red is excited about returning to Japan, but I would like to clarify my position. I will bring him as I did before even if it includes going to Dallas again. However, I will not be responsible if he acts in an unprofessional manner." In the final analysis, I decided it would be too risky.

When Red passed away on April 23, 1984, I organized a two-day festival in tribute to him. The following poem, printed on the program, conveys my feelings about him.

Dear Red:

You are like a beautiful flower that can blossom into bouquets of blue gardenias or gladiolas at will, whenever you played the piano. You always make me think of your favorite lyrics from the song "You leave me breathless."

Song quote excluded [Author's Note]

We are at loss for words when we try to describe how you warmed our hearts; and when you played the piano, every one of us understood every word you played.

From all of us here today, peace and love.

We're missing you terribly,

Jamil

PHINEAS NEWBORN

Journalist, Hollie West: "The other night Newborn 45, was still performing with the technical brilliance and musical verve that characterized his early playing. However, his once light touch has become more percussive. Bassist Marshal Hawkins and drummer Bernard Sweetney often looked at the pianist with their mouths open in amazement."[157]

"In 1978, after an 18-year absence, Phineas appeared at the Village Gate. Mr. Newborn, who has not lost any of the dazzling proficiency he commanded in the 50's was looking forward to coming back for some time. This writer [Robert Palmer] first encountered Mr. Newborn during the summer of 1975. Mr. Newborn gave an informal recital for a group of music students at Memphis State University and stayed afterward to answer questions about jazz and about his career."[158]

Anyone who doubts the veracity of this review need only listen to Phineas on Cybill Shepherd's album Vanilla (1978). During the obscure periods commonly referred to in Newborn's mini-biographies, he was willing and available to work.

For example, he appeared with Herbie Hancock, Chick Corea, Jay McShann, John Lewis, and Hank Jones at the 1979 Montreux Jazz Festival. Tenor saxophonist Fred Ford recalls: "At the end of the last set,

Hancock and Corea were reduced to beating on the wood of their Bosie because Little David the Giant Killer, the Albert Einstein of the piano had the keys sewed up." In addition, Fred claimed, "Months later, I heard that Atlantic's attempts to release the piano summit were stymied by representatives of some of the pianists who'd played with Junior. If this is true, it's understandable, because none of their careers would be enhanced by the evidence of how completely they were outplayed."[159]

A 1982 interview with Phineas:

Reese: You disappeared from the jazz scene in the sixties?

Phineas: Yes, I settled on the West Coast, and I played in Japan from time to time. I do not like to travel.

Reese: Do you come to Europe often?

Phineas: No, not in this age, but I came to Antibes in 1979 and had a good time. I particularly appreciate the European public. Unlike Japan or Europe, the Americans see music as a background thing, except in Los Angeles; they take music seriously.

Reese: How were your Contemporary discs recorded?

Phineas: The producer Les Koenig chose the rhythm section. I really love working with Elvin Jones; he is one of my favorite drummers. Our record Harlem Blues sold many copies in Japan. It was deeply rooted in the blues and spirituals.

Reese: Are you under contract to Pablo?

Phineas: When I left Contemporary, I was looking for a new record company. I played with Ray Brown in Los Angeles for a moment, and he encouraged Norman Granz to sign me to Pablo. Previously, I made a solo disk on Atlantic that was nominated for a Grammy.

Reese: What did you do in the meantime?

Phineas: I am under contract to record an album in Japan. I am very picky regarding my records and did not want to record—for a long time. I need to compose and learn the songs of other musicians. Now,

I want to record, and I will make a record that sells many copies. You will see!

Reese: In clubs, do you play more standards than original songs?

Phineas: I believe to reach an audience you must play music they can recognize... Americans don't understand new songs, so I play a lot of bebop, themes like 'Night in Tunisia.'

Reese: In your way of playing, I heard the influence of Art Tatum and Southern Blues?

Phineas: Yes, something like that, I try to combine the two: the way in which Tatum solved technical problems and the contribution of bop, Bud Powell, and Charlie Parker. Unfortunately, I never met Art Tatum. But I sent Art some of my recordings. Tatum said, 'I was one of the more interesting young pianists.' I went on tour with Bud Powell and could hear and play with him. He played well in spite of physical problems.

Reese: What about the blues pianists?

Phineas: I like boogie-woogie pianists like Pete Johnson and Albert Ammons.

Reese: When you lived in California at the end of the fifties, did you sense a difference between West Coast pianists and those in your hometown, Memphis?

Phineas: My favorite West Coast pianist was Hampton Hawes. And Les McCann was formidable before his commercial period.

Reese: What were your difficulties during the sixties?

Phineas: I did not want to perform in clubs, only concert halls. I managed to survive. In addition, I had some health problems, which is the reason I left New York. I got married in Los Angeles and did some teaching: I had some notable students, which include Harold Mabern, Charles Thomas, and James Williams. They asked me to do a concert in Boston.

REVIEW

In 1981, Phineas performed at the Berklee Performance Center: "Absent from this city for 20 years, according to host Tony Cennamo, Newborn made up for lost time with an unusually choppy, strident version of Horace Silver's 'Juicy Lucy,' that also contained some feisty high-octave yells. With a brief nod to Charlie Parker, he approached 'All the Things You Are' in a gently swinging fashion, laced with ascending runs and choruses that alternatively whispered and shouted. A standing ovation followed. 'Daahoud' danced along lightly into 'Willow Weep for Me' and the Memphis master, whose dexterity and speed makes him the only man Oscar Peterson fears, strode smartly on the finale, 'Just in Time.' A four-minute standing ovation this time trailed the Memphis master behind the curtain, only to return with the others for a share of the Summit cum laude.[160]

Reese: What was so special about Memphis?

Phineas: The blues is everywhere and it's used constantly. When musicians leave Memphis for other horizons, they never lose their identity. The blues in Memphis has a particular feeling, a slow blues. In the North, they play blues at a faster pace. In Memphis, we play low down, dirty blues, and sometimes sad blues.

Reese: What projects do you have in mind?

I really want to play with Max Roach. I had the opportunity to record with some great drummers like Kenny Clarke, Philly Joe Jones, Elvin Jones, Louis Hayes, etc. My father was a drummer, so I always had a passion for this instrument. I would like to have a trio with Ray Brown and Max Roach. And above all, I would like to do an album of spirituals with a chorus, an organist, and myself on piano.

Reese: You do not often play with brass?

Phineas: No, I play trumpet and tenor myself, so I could record using these instruments. It may be too late now, because I am older, and my cheeks are too flabby. When I was younger, my family had a great orchestra. We traded instruments. My brother played guitar and trombone; his wife sang, and played various instruments.

Reese: You have been considered a pianist with formidable technique. Are you a genius?

Phineas: I appreciate the compliment. It is nice to be called a genius; I do not fool around with music. I take my music very seriously.

Reese: Is it difficult to combine technique and creativity?

Phineas: Blues is one of the most intriguing types of music; it is fascinating to play. I use technique as a means to tell my story . . . I hate using technique for its own sake.

Reese: Did you study classical music as a youngster?

Phineas: Yes, I play it only to help me express myself in jazz. I used a Sonata by Ravel as an intro to Lush Life, because I find a lot of common points between both writers.

Reese: Who are your favorite pianists?

Phineas: Oscar Peterson is one of my favorites. I love George Shearing, Charles Thomas, and Keith Jarrett. Chick Corea is a great electric pianist. I find young musicians lack control. By the way, I forgot Stevie Wonder; he is extremely popular for using electric pianos. "You are the Sunshine of My Life" is a simple yet great song. The piano made great advances in the sixties. Some of those developments are used today. The keyboard has progressed tremendously in the last 20 years. I want to offer the public music that they can follow without overwhelming their minds too much. These are my ideas on the music.

Reese: Would you like to speak about your activities in the Seventies?

Phineas: I was in the hospital for long periods ... I was ill ... It gave me an opportunity to compose and practice my music. I am not ashamed of my past. I don't believe in the opinions of others.[161]

I saved the above interview as proof of Phineas' lucidity, despite rumors to the contrary.

Phineas, Frank Gant, and I had a rehearsal at Sweet Basil, in 1984, and one of the managers interrupted us, "Those cymbals sound terrible."

I asked him, "What the fuck are you talking about?"

"Do you know more about music than us?"

I asked Phineas, "How do the cymbals sound to you?"

"They sound fine to me." He said.

I told him, "People absorb sound: the cymbals will sound different during the performance. We don't tell you how to mix drinks . . . let us do our jobs."

He said, "I stand corrected."

But the next time Phineas appeared at Sweet Basil, they hired another bassist, so I took a gig with Kenny Burrell in Jamaica. The night before I left, the same manager called me and said, "Phineas plays short sets, wanders around the club, and takes long breaks." "Are you still available?" I said, "No, I have a gig in Jamaica. I suggest you called Frank Gant; he has a good rapport with Phineas." They followed my recommendation, and Phineas completed the week without further incident.[162]

John Wilson observed, "He had become an orchestral-minded, two-handed pianist who worked with melodies rather than lines of single notes, a habit he has retained. He also differs from his contemporaries because of his youthful experience playing for rhythm and blues singers."[163]

Author's Note: Phineas played a solo piano concert for the Red Garland tribute. Zaid and I stayed with Dad to help promote the concert. We slept on the floor, and Phineas slept on the bed. His determination to give a great concert permeated the atmosphere. Phineas would rise intermittently throughout the night, play some amazing music, have a hearty laugh, and return to bed.

The next morning, I arose to the pungent scent of marijuana and the sound of Here Is Phineas. Phineas was smoking a joint and listening to the album. I asked the rhetorical question, "What are you smoking?" He passed me the joint, and we listened to the rest of the album. As we prepared to leave, I played a chord on the piano, and Mr. Newborn gave me a chord voicing lecture that eluded my grasp. I tried for twenty minutes to hail a cab. Phineas had a sound check for his solo performance at the Jazz Center. When we arrived, Phineas took a seat at the piano and began to play. Mulgrew

Miller, Mickey Tucker, and James Williams were transfixed upon his every note. Then each pianist reserved a night to escort Phineas around town.

To give Phineas further inspiration, I took him to a concert that featured Oscar Peterson and Cecil Taylor. Phineas remained seated throughout Oscar's performance but didn't seem to appreciate Cecil's. I asked him about Taylor and he said, "I heard he was a bad cat, so I bought all of his records. You know, if he really wanted to be effective as an avant-garde pianist, I could teach him some obscure Ellington and Strayhorn compositions that sound free yet maintain the integrity of the piano."

Author's Review: After seeing old friends, hearing fellow musicians, and practicing around the clock, Phineas was ready to play. Cobi Narita announces "Ladies and gentlemen, Phineas Newborn Jr." Phineas introduces a five-part dance suite composed for his daughter "Rochella's Suite." His reading of "Lush Life" captures the mood of the piece; a fascinating introduction gives insight into his mastery of the European classical idiom à la Ravel. Next, he brilliantly interprets "Cherokee" in three different styles: ragtime, bebop, and European classical. The "Memphis Blues" transported us to Pee Wee's Saloon on Beale Street. And he closed with a ragtime/bebop interpretation of the "12th Street Rag." The crowd gave Phineas a much-deserved, two-minute standing ovation. The encore was a fast, intense version of "C Jam Blues."

The concert was a smashing success, and anyone who attended can confirm that Phineas was well-dressed, well-spoken, and played well. He displayed no sign of mental disability, the common pretext evoked to explain Newborn's underexposure.

On our last European tour, in 1988, I asked Phineas, "Is there anything that you have yet to accomplish in music?" He replied, "I would like to do an album of spirituals and write a symphony." Phineas had mastered the old Gospel Pearl Hymnal, which contained hieroglyphic type inscriptions. He played an arrangement of the "Lord's Prayer." Now, I have heard many versions, but his was so hauntingly beautiful. I told him, "If the gospel music world hears that . . . they will forever change their approach to "The Lord's Prayer."

James Williams and I worked hard to secure bookings. And Phineas often called me to see if any work was forthcoming. Unfortunately, his calendar remained empty, and the world lost the final creative thoughts of a musical genius.

Author's Note: On May 26, 1989, Phineas Newborn left the stage. A genius boycotted for demanding respect and self-ownership. Nevertheless, he died a proud man who made an indelible mark on African American music. His story is an admixture of triumph and tragedy. The industry may have circumscribed his opportunities, but they didn't completely thwart his efforts. His music still inspires musicians—especially pianists—around the world.

LOU DONALDSON AND SOUTH AFRICA

I once introduced Lou as follows: "In history we have very important people, some great people, and some unusual people. This next gentleman qualifies in all categories, a man who knows the whole spectrum of jazz from Louis Armstrong all the way up. He has recorded jazz and soul masterpieces. This man lives to swing; let's welcome the incomparable Lou Donaldson."

Journalist, Owen McNally: "Just back from Scandinavia, the [Lou Donaldson] quartet played as a tightly knit group—a genuine working band rather than the lose sort of aggregation (or aggravation) that sometimes wind their way through Hartford. Musically, the most valuable figure in the quartet was bassist Jamil Nasser, a musician that worked many years in pianist Ahmad Jamal's celebrated trio. Nasser is a most melodious, inventive, and witty improviser, one whose solos sounded like song forms that could stand entirely on their own as little works of art. Nasser was full of surprises. Light fleet dancing figures alternated with dark sonorous, low register colorations, and allusions to other tunes rippled gracefully through his choruses. When not soloing, he tended most skillfully to his time keeping duties."[164]

Lou Donaldson: "In the '60s, after playing a gig in Kansas City, we went to the musicians' union, and observed a wall with the photos of Kansas City musicians, but there was no photo of Charlie Parker. When we questioned the union reps about this glaring omission, they said, the union president didn't appreciate Parker because of his drug addiction. Jamil and I purchased a picture of Bird and placed it on the wall."

In September 1981, the Don Hughes Organization invited Lou Donaldson and Dakota Staton to South Africa. Lou offered me the gig, and I accepted. We played ten concerts.

Author's Note: South Africa in the early eighties: "By the 1980's, South Africa had become quite isolated from International cultural and sporting arenas. In the early eighties, the United Nations declared it would blacklist any performer who traveled to South Africa. Essentially, the UN cultural boycott meant that there would be no exchange between performers or performances between that country and the rest of the world."[165]

"Jazz artist Chick Corea has got the blues. Claiming special status as an 'artist and a communicator,' Corea performed his magical music in apartheid South Africa last year in violation of repeated calls for a boycott of the white minority regime. But back home, the anti-apartheid movement did a little communicating of its own picketing Corea in Albany, New York, and at one of the Greenwich Village clubs, the Village Vanguard. The two pickets, following closely on the heels of similar protests against the O'Jays, Ray Charles, Lou Donaldson, and Candi Staton this past fall, are an indication that performers tempted to perform in the white supremacist country must now seriously weigh the political and financial consequences of accepting such a gig.

To date, the effort has been spearheaded by two Black community organizations based in New York. These are the Unity Action Network, founded by the Harlem based Patrice Lumumba Coalition and the African Jazz Artist Society and Studios, and the Coalition to End Cultural Collaboration with South Africa, formed in response to a call from the National Black United Front (NBUF) for a Black reply to artists—particularly Black artists who violate the international cultural embargo.

Elobe Brath, the leader of the Patrice Lumumba Coalition said, 'There is no excuse for being uninformed in 1982,' Brath observed. 'But we give them the benefit of the doubt. We want to work with these people. We are not trying to intimidate anybody; we trying to make them see the light. We think this can be a very good organizing tool, a process of raising people's consciousness about the situation in South Africa—to try to inform these musicians and the general public.'" [166]

ABC employed Elobe Brath, one of the boycott leaders; who assisted Gil Noble, the producer of *Like It Is.* ABC had investments in South Africa. So Elobe should have started his protest by submitting his resignation.

I defied the cultural boycott to seek first-hand information on South Africa. I didn't buy the argument that we shouldn't go because of the institutional racism there; I played segregated venues throughout the South in '40s and '50s.

The honorary white status on our travel documents prevented problems with the South African authorities. And we performed for integrated audiences in Sun City and other cities. Many of the indigenous South Africans asked me why we didn't come there more often, so I explained the boycott to them. They told us how one record would circulate throughout a community.

The South Africans I spoke with said, "We are better off than African Americans, because we will regain control of our country once apartheid is dismantled." Our concert tour was successful, and I left convinced that South Africa would emerge as a viable market for our music in the post-apartheid era.

HOWARD "DUKE" ANDERSON

Author's Note: My father respected the artistry and wisdom of the late, great pianist Duke Anderson. Although, I didn't intend to include this section. The scant information on the internet obligated me to do so. In 1992, Mr. Anderson wrote this brief historical sketch: I was born in 1915. I played in carnivals throughout America from 1929-1932. Then, in 1934, I joined Chick Webb's band and prepared copy arrangements for Don Redmond. It thrilled me to play in the first bands of Dizzy Gillespie, Tiny Bradshaw, and Ike Quebec. Ike's band had me, Oscar Pettiford on bass, and Shadow Wilson on drums. We had a regular engagement at the Three Deuces on 52nd Street.

In 1949, I played with Charlie Parker at the St. George Hotel in Montreal. His pianist didn't show, so he asked me to play. He called "Cherokee" and started playing some atonal figures, so I followed him. When he finished the set, he said, "I didn't want you to move with me. I wanted you to stay where you were and let me do the moving." I learned that a pianist can interfere with a soloist.

In 1934, I had just closed in Chillicothe, Ohio. Back in those days, black performers stayed in tourist homes. One morning, I heard someone playing breathtaking piano. And I followed the sound and introduced myself to a man named Art Tatum. Art had heard about me playing with a towel over my hands. He said, "That's so degrading, I'm going to show you how to play." He taught me all the tricks like how to make an arpeggio with three fingers. I wrote a book called New Adventures in Harmony, which contains some concepts I learned from him. No jazz historian ever asked me about Art Tatum, and I knew more about him than anybody.

Because of the many traps in the music business, I opted to perform on a part-time basis; however, I had private students and wrote big band arrangements. Moreover, I worked as Count Basie's substitute from 1972 until he passed in 1984.[167]

MONTY ALEXANDER

Monty is a great pianist with a fantastic concept and ear. I took him to see Duke Anderson. Mr. Anderson told me, "I don't find it necessary to teach Monty the formulas as his conception contains them naturally."

Monty Alexander: "I played "Come Sunday" for Duke; he loved my interpretation of the song. His compliment meant more than anything a critic or reviewer may write about me."

I used to visit Jamil on 293 Central Park West, a building that housed great musicians like Les Spann, the brilliant guitarist, flautist, and saxophonist Jerome Richardson. I met his wife Karimah and witnessed the arrival of his children. We had many extended conversations on music, women, religion, and boxing. We were avid boxing fans, so I bought tickets for us to see Muhammad Ali and Ken Norton fight at Yankee Stadium.

On December 31, 1978, Jamil and I established a publishing company called Monass Music Inc. Jamil had a great mind for business and taught me about music publishing. My song "Unlimited Love" (renamed "Sweet Lady") was recorded by Oscar Peterson, and I recorded "Tropical Breeze" by Jamil Nasser, both songs were published by Monass.

In 1979, we performed at Rosy's in New Orleans with Milt Jackson on vibes, Jamil on bass and Frank Gant on drums. Moreover, we performed in Vancouver, BC; Aix-en-Provence, France; Montreux, Switzerland; and London, England.

Jamil taught me many lessons about life, politics, religion, and the music industry. He had a penchant for seeking out great pianists. He introduced me to Oscar Dennard through private recordings. I heard him support Ahmad Jamal, Al Haig, Dorothy Donegan, and Eddie Heywood. Jamil and Eddie had a long-standing engagement at Jimmy Weston's on 52nd Street. The respect and deference Jamil displayed towards Heywood and Donegan warmed my heart. Mrs. Donegan was one of the greatest pianists to grace the instrument. She received an endorsement from her hero, Art Tatum, and invoked fear in ninety-nine percent of the jazz pianists. I love the orchestral pianists like Art Tatum, Oscar Peterson, Erroll Garner, Phineas Newborn, and Ahmad Jamal. The bebop and soul pianists were great; however, the virtuoso pianists had the greatest influence on me.

Ahmad's trio with Jamil and Frank was a tight ensemble; they shared a special bond tempered by life—its joys and struggles. And they faced challenges in Suriname and other places. I would show up to see them in the Midwest or Buffalo. They would ask, "What are you doing here?" Ahmad and Jamil carried themselves with dignity and didn't tolerate foolishness. Some people expect musicians to walk through the back door. I have observed the fine line that exists between musicians and artists. An artist must command respect; we are here to uplift the people with music, which requires confidence and peace of mind.

For example, in April 1981, we had a two-week engagement at Ronnie Scott's in London. My quartet included my early mentor and master guitarist Ernest Ranglin, Jamil on bass, and Frank Gant on drums. Jamil counseled me on how to resolve an incident at our sound check. A spotlight obstructed my vision, so I asked the lighting technician to adjust it. One of the owners heard my complaint and said, "Well, you know, we're in show business, and the audience must see you." His disrespectful attitude and tone had me fuming. Then Jamil leaned over and said, "Don't allow anymore air to leak through those cracks." I got up, walked up to him, and said, "Don't you ever address me like that again; I must create proper working conditions for my band, respect me." I read him the riot act. When I arrived for the gig, the man I upbraided earlier approached me in the lobby and apologized with tears in his eyes. Jamil had issued a statement and directive simultaneously. And the message was loud and clear: If you tolerate a little disrespect, then more is sure to follow.

Frank hung out in Brixton one afternoon before work and expressed concern about the unrest brewing there. The next day, we awoke to breaking news about the Brixton riots.

We performed at the 1988 Montreux Jazz Festival. I invited Jamil to be part of the "Ivory and Steel" Tour (1991). The nine-piece ensemble performed in nine English cities. "This is the Jazz of the 1990's, a jazz ride around the Caribbean, with plenty of surprises."[168]

While I do appreciate, the younger musicians playing now, when I came on the scene in the early '60s, the great musicians had a personal voice. I could identify Art Blakey or Philly Joe Jones after hearing four bars, because they had a unique fingerprint that was unmistakable. In the 1970s, a new generation of college-educated musicians emerged and it became more difficult to identify individual artists.

Jamil had a unique bass style, which projects the Memphis blues influence. In addition, he had a great stroke, an incredible ear for harmony, and musical sensibilities shaped by supporting masters like Red Garland, Oscar Dennard, Phineas Newborn, and Ahmad Jamal. When we played together . . . it was like a party![169]

Papa Jo Jones

Papa Jo had an amazing memory, so when Albert Murray interviewed Count Basie, Basie told him to consult Papa Jo.

When Albert came for the interview, Papa Jo said, "Before we get started is the title going to be "The Story of Count Basie as told to Albert Murray by Jonathan David Samuel Jones?"

Albert said, "I will be the sole author."

Papa Jo said, "I can't remember shit," and faced the wall.

I came to visit Papa Jo one night and he said, "I want you to take me somewhere!"

I didn't bother to ask where or why.

He got in the car, and said, "Fat Tuesday's."

We walked in the door. He spotted Ray Brown and yelled, "Ray Brown, come here!"

Ray shrugged his shoulders and tiptoed up to him.

Papa Jo said, "I came here tonight, because I want give you something." He slowly pulled out his wallet and handed him a card.

He said, "I want you to take this card and read it sometime."

The card asked the following question, "Have you helped someone today?"

Then he turned to me and said, 'Let's go!'

I remember him admiring the talent of a great young drummer named Clifford Jarvis. He wanted to share some esoteric drum wisdom: the kind of special information reserved for choice students. He gave a demonstration and explanation, then, Clifford said, dismissively, "Man, I can do that!" Papa Jo replied, "It took me thirty-five years to learn that, but you can do it after one viewing?" It was his first and last lesson.

Papa Jo often said, "Where did it all go?" He constantly looked over the horizon for young talent but didn't see many promising young musicians. One time, Ringo Starr came by Frank Ippolito's drum shop, and Papa Jo handed him a pair of drumsticks and said, "I heard you're the greatest drummer in the world." "Play me a drum roll." Ringo got up outta there, quick.

In Paris, he suddenly announced, I must be on the next flight to New York. Madame Turez told him it would be too expensive without reservations. He yelled, "I must be on the next plane to New York!" Basie passed while Papa Jo was en route. He said, "I had to be there to hold Freddie Green up and vice versa. Basie turned over five times in his grave, because the people he wanted inside were outside."

Author's Note: In June 1984, my father sent me and Zaid to meet Papa Jo. Mr. Jones told us, "I just canceled my gig at the West End." 'Why?' I asked. And he said, "I am tired of fattening frogs for snakes." When I raised the subject of Billie Holiday's drug addiction, he asked me, "Did you ever see her using drugs?" Initially, I thought he was being sarcastic; however, the rationale for his question crystallized months later. I made statement about Mrs. Holiday instead of asking a question. He said, "There are three people I don't allow anyone to fuck with: Mr. Lester Young, Mrs. Billie Holiday, and Mr. Count Basie."'

I mustered up the courage to ask him about his personal experiences with racism. Unfortunately, I struck a sensitive chord and a furious anger emerged which caused the veins in his baldhead to swell. Then he screamed,

"Don't ask me that shit . . . don't ask me that fuckin' shit. We had to endure those struggles that you might live!" His visceral response spoke louder than words.

Papa Jo told me, "I never threw a cymbal at Charlie Parker in Kansas City." Furthermore, he expressed a desire to challenge the author of this myth.

He said, "Before my benefit at the Village Gate (A Love Letter to Papa Jo), I called Max Roach and told him to play after Philly Joe. Philly Joe Jones is the greatest natural drummer that ever lived."

His motto was "The drum is to be played not beaten." Papa Jo could achieve a high level of intensity without volume. He gave me two books: "The Autobiography of Malcolm X" and a biography of the brilliant pianist Thomas Greene Bethune (aka Blind Tom). He had an archive of newspaper articles, rare records, and photos; unfortunately, a fire in his apartment destroyed them. His final statement, "The next time you come here, bring a tape recorder, and make it soon." Unfortunately, he expired before I could return.

HANK MOBLEY

In 1985, I played one of Hank's last gigs in Philly. He was in bad shape physically and would play a short phrase then run to the bathroom. It broke my heart to see him like this. When he died the following year, Donald Byrd told me, "Hank's funeral was sad . . . only a handful of people were there."

SONNY STITT

I performed with Sonny Stitt at Beefsteak Charlie's in 1982. He had to sit in a chair, because he was drinking heavily. The pianist struggled with the music. But Sonny didn't want to cast blame upon her, so he turned to me and said, "Hey man, what are you doing?" I leaned over and said in his ear, 'I'm a fucking professional, respect me.' He said, "Alright, baby."' It hurt me to have this contentious exchange with Sonny. He expired shortly after this gig.

The confluence of Reaganomics, disco, hip-hop, and punk rock made the eighties a challenging period for jazz artists. Thus, I had to develop an independent approach to presenting the music.

12

The Kings Series

I don't wait for the industry to promote me.

–*Jamil Nasser*

Kings Series Mission Statement 1980

The Kings Series aims to perpetuate the jazz art, without cliques, props, costumes, or the narrow limitations imposed by the industry and academia. Kings are master artists who should be leading the jazz community.

Festival organizers assemble jazz groups without regard for musical compatibility, which results in lackluster performances. The Kings Series presents artists in compatible combinations of trios, quartets, quintets, octets, and big bands. In addition, we give lectures, demonstrations, concerts, festivals, and jazz revues. Consequently, we can offer our patrons exciting events that draw upon our historical and musical connection to Louis Armstrong, Art Tatum, Charlie Parker, Lester Young, Duke Ellington, and Count Basie et al.

KINGS SERIES CONCERTS

I booked an all-star group that included Junior Cook on tenor sax, Kenny Drew on piano, Sam Jones on bass, and Jimmy Cobb on drums for a 1981 Japanese tour. Sam was ill, and a Japanese doctor drained a copious amount of fluid from his lungs: he expired shortly after this tour. My friend and associate, Cobi Narita, the Director of the Universal Jazz Coalition, staged many of our concerts and workshops at her venue, the Jazz Center of New York. Moreover, she supported the great women artists (vocalists and instrumentalists) by presenting them at the Jazz Center and later Cobi's Place.

I staged a tribute to Red Garland on June 29-30, 1984—the same week as the Kool Jazz Festival. On May 17–19, 1985, the Kings Series in collaboration with the Presbyterian Jazz Society produced the Westchester Jazz Festival, which featured Curtis Fuller, Junior Cook, Bill Hardman, and Phineas Newborn. On June 6, 1987, I organized a musical celebration of three great bassists: Walter Page, Oscar Pettiford, and Israel Crosby, which featured five bassoons and a four-piece rhythm section. It was an opportunity to compose and arrange for the bassoon, which is rarely heard in a jazz context.

In addition, The United Nations Jazz Society asked me to bring a group to the UN. On November 20, 1987, we performed as the Joe Newman Sextet, which included Joe Newman and Irvin Stokes on trumpet, Frank Wess on tenor sax, Harold Mabern on piano, Frank Gant on drums, and me on bass.

In 1989, I organized a Japanese tour with Joe Newman, Harold Mabern, Frank Gant, and me. When I booked all-star groups, I insisted upon equal billing and pay for each musician. I won't itemize each Kings Series concert; the advertisements included in this text speak for themselves. I later changed the name of organization from the Kings Series to Global Arts International Inc.

GEORGE COLEMAN/TENOR SAXOPHONE SHOOTOUTS

I can't remember when George couldn't play. If you listen to his solo on B.B. King's "Woke Up This Morning," you'll hear early manifestations of his brilliance.

I have great respect for his artistry. Playing with him required the utmost in physical and mental preparation, because he is a genius in every sense of the word . . . the heavyweight champion of the tenor saxophone, who can play any key, tempo, or groove. Frank Foster sat in with us at the Village Vanguard and George played "Mack The Knife" in every key—fast. After the set, Frank told me, "It took all the harmonic, arranging, and saxophone skills I developed over forty-years to make it through that set." Moreover, he's a great educator, in fact, George wrote out some great harmonic ideas for me to practice.

George Coleman: "Jamil's organization of the tenor shootout displayed saxophonists in a competitive context. And they challenged young artists and exposed media-crowned "heavyweights" by showcasing the true masters."[170]

Tenor saxophone battles were a consistent part of the Kings Series concerts. On January 15, 1979, I organized a historic tenor battle: "The Shootout on Eleventh Street."

Journalist, Richard Sudhalter: "Last night's 'Tenor Shootout on 11th Street' belonged, at least in name, to a long and deeply-etched jazz tradition. Organized by bassist Jamil Nasser under the aegis of the Universal Jazz Coalition, it featured Ricky Ford, Sal Nistico, Frank Wess, George Coleman, and Harold Vick. They worked in front of a gold-star rhythm team: Nasser on bass, pianist Tommy Flanagan, and drummer Ray Mosca in the auditorium of the Third Street Music School. Billing notwithstanding, the accent was less on competition than on camaraderie. Each soloist did two numbers by himself, generally an up-tempo swinger and a ballad or medium walker. Only at the end did the mix strike fire. The saxophonists filed up to take their turns on a spirited 'I'll Remember April,' whittling things down from multichoruses to eights to twos. With the rhythm section playing stops, the exchange became a conversation—witty, a little wicked. Sometimes phrases ran so seamlessly it was hard to tell who was playing."[171]

Author's Note: In June 1984, Clifford Jordan, Harold Vick, and George Coleman joined forces and played a furious, up-tempo version of "Lover" and "Blues Up and Down."

The "Tribute to Harold Vick" on February 6, 1988, culminated in a "Tenor Saxophone Summit" which featured Junior Cook, Jimmy Heath, Frank Wess, and George Coleman. These concerts, when released, will add much to the historical canon of tenor saxophone blowing sessions.

The Kings Series often presented the George Coleman Quartet. The rhythm section included Harold Mabern on piano, Jamil Nasser on bass, and/or Idris Muhammad, Frank Gant, Billy Higgins on drums. They took no prisoners. George would usually begin by playing a blazing up-tempo number. It wasn't uncommon for the quartet to play a song through the cycle of keys, and the solos were long and strong. The Memphis blues influence was ever-present in their interpretation of standards, Broadway show tunes, bebop, or a Stevie Wonder classic.

George Coleman: "We grew up in Memphis together, jamming at the Mitchell Hotel and playing gigs around town. In 1955, we toured the country with B.B. King's band. Jamil possessed an in-depth knowledge of harmony and played on a high-performance level in any key or tempo. In addition, he possessed a big tone and played great melodic solos full of personality, humor, intelligence, and emotion. Although small in stature, Jamil had a tremendous amount of endurance and stamina."[172]

In an interview with Ted Pankin, George said, "Fortunately, when I am playing, that's basically when I'm practicing, when I'm trying to create new things or do new things, and just relax and play. If I have players like Idris and Jamil and Geoff and Harold Mabern and people like that, that's the motivation. It gives me incentive to try new things and create new things. Because I don't have to think about whether the beat is going to be messed up or somebody is going to play some wrong changes. All I have to do is lay back and just play, and when I am able to do this, I can come up with some creativity."[173]

Author's Note: The album, Manhattan Panorama, captures the George Coleman Quartet in the mid-eighties. The recording explores a wide range of musical angles. "Subway Ride" is an up-tempo E-flat blues that captures the swiftness of the A Train whisking a rider from 59th to 125th Street. "The New York Housing Blues" gives the listener a healthy dose of the Memphis blues. "The New York Suite" features brilliant renditions of standards and show tunes related to New York.

Journalist, Herb Boyd: "It was a formidable buzz, and very few of the evening's all-star musicians could cut through the din of laughter, schmoozing, and good cheer. Tenor saxophonist George Coleman and his quartet not only slashed through the noisy conversations but also took them to another level of excitement. After a raucous blues tune with his sax stretched to the musical breaking point, Coleman lit into a charged-up version of "Strike Up the Band," which drummer Frank Gant, bassist Jamil Nasser and pianist Harold Mabern took as a command, laying a hot rhythmic cinder path for their leader. Coleman hop-stepped over the burning intensity, shaping the song's heat to his own quite expansive dictates."[174]

George called upon the skills of the late, great trumpeter and flugelhornist Danny Moore for quintet and octet engagements. Peter Watrous reviewed Danny's 1992 performance at the Vanguard: "The trumpeter Danny Moore isn't much of a household name, and for whatever reason, Mr. Moore has stayed outside the club and recording circuit and the publicity that goes along with it. The reason can't be his playing. His solos exemplify the ability of mainstream jazz to be charged by a genuinely improvisational personality. His playing comes from the mid-50's trumpet lexicon, but the way he phrases and all the embellishments he uses, made his improvisation swell with meaning."[175]

The Village Vanguard regularly featured the George Coleman Quartet. Max Gordon, the late, owner of the Village Vanguard, loved us. One night at the Vanguard, actress and director, Penny Marshall, invited George Coleman, Ted Dunbar, Roy Haynes, and me to act in a club scene supporting Whitney Houston and Denzel Washington in the motion picture *The Preacher's Wife*. Lionel Richie played the piano in our scene. We had a wonderful conversation concerning the importance of jazz preservation. He wanted to perform at "A Great Night in Harlem," the Jazz Foundation's annual fundraising concert.

The Kings Series enabled me to work independently, and thus employ musicians overlooked by the industry, which rides jazz artists like mules to fortune only to cast them aside poverty stricken with no health insurance or pension plan. Papa Jo Jones, the modern drum pioneer, was one of those artists.

The same man who I witnessed in healthier days cutting down the greatest drummers on the planet with just a hi-hat and a pair of sticks.

Drummer, Louis Bellson: "At a jam session in 1968 at the Newport Jazz Festival, with Buddy Rich, Elvin Jones, Mel Lewis, Roy Haynes, and other great drummers, I did everything I could with two bass drums. Elvin played real well. Everybody just—boom—played hard and creatively. Came time for Jo Jones, he went out with a hi-hat and a pair of sticks and tore everybody apart. We all threw up our hands and said, "OK, you got it man. That's all. No drum set, just a hi-hat. And he broke it up."[176]

13

THE JAZZ FOUNDATION OF AMERICA

"The bass player Jamil Nasser is on our board," said the foundation's current president Leo Corbie. He always said that he's not interested in museums; he's interested in the living.

It was Ms. Reid's friend Jamil Nasser, vice-president of the Jazz Foundation, who saw to it that the singer was given free car service from her Bronx home to the New Jersey Hospital. She also has received extensive tests and specialist services. "Many jazz musicians," Nasser said, "have fallen on hard times."

As mentioned earlier, Papa Jo's advice saved my life, so I looked out for him in his twilight years. For instance, when he was ill, I went to the hospital every day, and the administrators started asking about his health insurance. I told them the policy was buried somewhere in his apartment, which worked for a couple weeks. But they soon issued an ultimatum: "If we don't have those insurance papers by tomorrow, we will discharge him." I called Vi Redd in California, and she got right on it. The next day, I returned to the hospital and the nurse told me, "Everything is ok; a famous singer, who prefers to remain anonymous, agreed to cover the expenses." I believe Frank Sinatra stepped up to the plate to assist Papa Jo.

On April 23, 1982, I organized a much-needed fundraiser for Papa Jo at the Village Gate: "A Love Letter to Papa Jo." His table sat just a couple of feet from the drums. And the top purveyors of the instrument, which included Mel Lewis, Philly Joe Jones, Max Roach, Idris Muhammad, Art Taylor, and Billy Higgins played drum solos for him. The event raised 15,000 dollars to defray the cost of medical and living expenses. The unity and love among those musicians was inspiring. I organized and supported many fundraisers for poverty-stricken musicians, so I knew the Jazz Foundation could play an integral role in addressing this issue.

In 1989, the passing of Phineas Newborn, who lacked the funds for a proper burial, fueled the creation of the Jazz Foundation of America. The founders were Herb Storfer, Billy Taylor, Cy Blank, Ann Ruckert, and Phoebe Jacobs. The President, Herb Storfer, was a musician and jazz archivist at the New York Public Library's Schomberg Center for Research and Black Culture.

As the vice president and a member of the executive committee, I reminded my associates that jazz musicians have been thrown out to the wolves for a long time; it's a pitiful state. Jazz is a national treasure, but what's the point if we do not take care of the treasures? These treasures are becoming like snail darter. In 1992, we established the Jazz Musicians Emergency Fund to aid musicians facing financial difficulty due to illness or lack of work.

Trumpeter, Jimmy Owens: "The Jazz Foundation's primary concern was preserving the legacy of dead musicians. Jamil Nasser, Vishnu Wood, and I changed their focus, because we wanted the organization to support living artists."[177]

The following mission statement reflects our influence on the organization:

"The Jazz Foundation of America is committed to providing financial, medical, and legal assistance to those great blues and jazz veterans who have paid their dues by making a lifetime of music and find themselves

in crisis due to illness, age, and/or circumstance. The Jazz Foundation of America is further committed to act as a blues and advocacy organization; to advance the knowledge and appreciation of jazz music and jazz organizations; and to afford the public an opportunity to hear performances by some of the creators of the music themselves and keep them working and performing in the process."

The late Herb Storfer, former JFA President observed: *"Many have died penniless, their families bankrupted by medical and other unplanned expenses, for jazz musicians have special problems unique to their craft. As 'freelancers' they rarely belong to a stable organization year-round. Thus, they do not usually qualify for health insurance, pensions, and other benefits. In reality, the musician's union classifies them as 'casual musicians,' who are therefore not eligible for most benefits. Also, since most jazz clubs are barely profitable, jazz musicians are placed in a poor bargaining position, and often play for marginal fees. When one adds the pressures of playing one-nighters on the road, it is understandable why all too many jazz musicians are prey to health problems. The Jazz Musicians Emergency Fund cares and is doing everything it can to alleviate these problems."*[178]

Jimmy Owens: *"In 1959, the musician's union created a pension fund, but it was a deep, dark secret. Jazz musicians were not aware of its existence until the '60s. "When we talk about jazz, we see musicians, who have been masters all their lives, and because of the areas they have worked in, they have not been able to build pension funds for themselves or hospitalize themselves. But musicians who have worked in Broadway theaters or the symphony orchestras had these benefit programs for them through the union. I've played so many benefits to aid people in their hospital costs, if not bury them, and I am tired of doing that. One of Dizzy Gillespie's last requests on this earth was to have Englewood Hospital treat musicians who lack health insurance. Dr. Francis Forte and Dr. Bob Litiwick agreed to head the Dizzy Gillespie Memorial Fund. I organized an event called "100 Trumpets for Dizzy."*[179]

Vocalist Irene Reid grappled with heart and thyroid problems. And she had no medical insurance. *"When Jamil told me, 'Irene, you're gonna get the best medical care, all the help you really need, and it won't cost you a penny,' this is one of the best things that ever happened to me," Ms. Reid said of the health program. "I walked in and even though I said I had no insurance, everyone was beautiful to me. No questions asked. I thought he had to be kidding."180*

Teri Thornton, the gifted vocalist and favorite of Ella Fitzgerald, received medical assistance through the Jazz Foundation: "Thornton made a brief splash on the jazz scene in the early 1960s, recording three albums, one yielding the radio hit, "Somewhere in the Night (Theme from Naked City)." Then she disappeared- "I had the blues for 35 years," she joked, ruefully."181

In 1998, Teri began her battle with bladder cancer. She, like Irene, had no medical insurance, yet received free emergency surgery and chemotherapy treatments at Englewood Hospital.

Vocalist and pianist, Teri Thornton: "In the beginning, when I needed so much medical attention, they were able to subsidize me financially. And the whole purpose for the organization is to give help to jazz musicians who are over fifty and have no health insurance and have just about spent their lives playing or involving themselves in jazz. I certainly was eligible for that and my friend [Jamil Nasser, Vice President] was president of the organization at one time. He took me to the hospital that consented to treat patients that came under the heading as eligible for the Dizzy Gillespie Fund. That's how it all came about."182

Teri, a great vocalist and pianist whose style contains the combined influence of Sarah and Ella, was passed over. Teri sung the theme song for a popular television show until she said, "No!" and it doesn't matter what that no was about. In the music industry, a white list is maintained for brown people and a brown list for white people. You can get off the brown list . . . like the people in Hollywood . . . you never get off the white list, and that's why Teri was covered up.

Author's Note: Teri entered and won the 1998 International Thelonious Monk Vocal Competition. Moreover, she recorded I'll be Easy to Find on Verve before passing on May 2, 2000.

I wanted to influence Lucky Thompson's return to the jazz scene, and I used my office as the vice president of the Jazz

Foundation to revive his career. In fact, I wrote President Bill Clinton a letter to solicit his support, but he never responded. My efforts to help Lucky precipitated a conflict between me and Herb.

As an African American jazz musician, I confronted the same racism and frustration that prompted Lucky's withdrawal from the music business. So, I tailored my strategy accordingly, but Herb asked Lucky's daughter about my plans, and she told him, "I only feel comfortable discussing my father with Jamil." I confronted Herb about his backdoor inquiry about my plans and resigned my post as the vice president of the Jazz Foundation. Many musicians received assistance from the Jazz Foundation of America, and I was gratified to extend a helping hand to my fellow musicians.

JAZZ AS A NATIONAL TREASURE/ HR-57

On April 29, 1987, a bus filled with jazz musicians and jazz supporters traveled to Washington DC to support Congressman John Conyers' resolution HR-57, which designated jazz as a national treasure. We realized that jazz—America's only art form—evolved out of the African American experience. Furthermore, we emphasized that jazz was bordering on extinction as its greatest creators and exponents were passing away without recognition. The American media romanticizes the image of a struggling jazz artist whose constant companions are poverty and drug addiction.

On the other hand, European classical artists receive federal subsidies and private grants, and this support is critical to the preservation and proliferation of European classical music. Black caucus leader, Shirley Chisholm, pointed out that approximately ninety-seven percent of the federal funds are earmarked for European classical and only three percent for jazz. Ms. Chisholm concluded this situation was both illegal and unjust. Despite the media suppression and distortion of jazz, it has captured the imagination and hearts of people throughout the world.

I delivered a powerful message that dramatized the plight of jazz musicians. Mayday was the central theme of my address to the congressional committee.

I read aloud the names of great artists who had passed away within the last ten years and said, "We are making a mayday call to this august body: help us reconstruct and save the jazz art. We need this resolution to reconnect the jazz tree to its roots that it might once again blossom and grow.

The pyramids and sphinx captured the greatness of a people and served as an inspiration for future generations. In the jazz art, our monuments are great performances of artists captured on records, videos, and tapes. This legislation will affirm America's commitment to perpetuate its only original art form. Our music appeals to the higher sensibilities in the human soul; consequently, there was never a riot at a jazz festival or performance.

Like Mozart, our great geniuses: Lester Young, Phineas Newborn, Lucky Thompson, and Gigi Gryce were victims of artistic genocide, and no one yelled mayday! I personally witnessed the genocide of rhythm and blues. Today, we can make sure this history doesn't repeat itself; therefore, we appeal to you to pass this resolution. Our roots are in danger. It may already be too late, but we must try to rectify this situation. We owe it to our Creator and our beloved masters who gave us this beautiful art form."

The following three elements of Resolution HR-57 encapsulate my mission as an advocate for the preservation and perpetuation of jazz:

1. *This great American musical art form has not yet been properly recognized nor accorded the institutional status commensurate with its value and importance.*
2. *It is important for the youth of America to recognize and understand jazz as a significant part of their cultural and intellectual heritage.*

3. *Whereas, in as much as, there exists no effective national infrastructure to support and preserve jazz."*

Jazz preservation demands that elder musicians teach the next generation of artists. Lets' explore a few of my concepts, ideas, and experiences concerning jazz education.

14

PASSING THE BATON

Following intermission, there was an incredible demonstration and illustration of the rhythm section's role in jazz. Led by Jamil Nasser, it drew raves from the enthusiastic audience.

"The music industry is telling you what to think," Nasser said, "There are other things, other than rap." Nasser noted that jazz is the "highest form" of an African-American music evolution that began with gospel and blues. He criticized rap for its overreliance on the spoken word as opposed to singing, and for using electronic gimmicks such as sampling (the use of recorded music as background) to replace musicianship. He said the young musicians aren't learning the 'secrets' of how to make music. 'There's a silent competition among jazz musicians,' said Nasser, who has played in blues legend B.B. King's band. 'For us, playing is like the Olympics every night.' Nasser invited the audience to pick up records by Sarah Vaughan and Ella Fitzgerald, instead of rap records.

I met Jamil in Seattle in the late sixties and took several lessons with him. I expressed my ambivalence about going to New York to pursue a career as a jazz bassist. Jamil told me, 'No matter how big the pot, the cream always rises to the top.'

—RUFUS REID

I taught my students the blues provides a basic form, which allows an improviser to focus on storytelling and swinging. I had students who were obsessed with developing great technique at the expense of creativity and soul.

Ray Brown pulled my coat to the limitations of the technique only approach. I was practicing difficult bass exercises that required eighteen-hour practice sessions. And I wanted to impress Ray with my prodigious technique, so I went to see him at the Embers and he said, "Play something for me, I haven't heard you in a while." I grabbed his bass, played "Play Fiddle Play," and began soloing using pyrotechnics. Then he put his hand over mine on the bass and said, 'Wherever you are going with that . . . you are already there.'"

I always realized the importance of learning from the elders. They were the founding fathers who paid some heavy dues to lay the roots of our musical tree. And I would worry them to death seeking knowledge of jazz history.

When our elders hired us (not a record company putting us with them) . . . they came looking for us because we were qualified. When they accepted you, it only confirmed that you were on the right track. All of us had holes in our playing until we hit their bandstands. You can't do it without them as they possess the secrets. In short, the university of jazz is on the bandstand, on the streets, and in apprenticeships. I wouldn't fly with a pilot who hasn't served an apprenticeship, because I couldn't trust him to land or takeoff.

For example, in 1981, I conducted a seminar for Howard University students. Unfortunately, the professors chose an off-campus bar for the workshop and some students were drinking whiskey. I asked the professors to present their top students, and they couldn't play an F blues. I canceled the performance and lectured them. The students were so misinformed, I asked their teachers to play for me, but most of them left, except for one, who admitted he wasn't qualified to teach the students properly.

Tenor saxophonist, Atiba Taylor recalls: "We met at Mr. Y's on Rhode Island Avenue. One of the students called "Spain" by Chick Corea and fumbled over the melody. Jamil stopped the tune and said, "The composition is great but beyond your technical command, play something, you really know." He taught us "Never to sacrifice feeling at the altar of technique. Just because you can play some things . . . doesn't mean you're playing something." In addition, he stressed the importance of slow practice. Lastly, Jamil cautioned us against blind imitation. He said, "Don't be afraid to project your story through the music."[183]

Cheney Thomas, a bassist at Howard University, recalls "Jamil was a serious taskmaster."I received one of the few compliments he gave. He said, "I had a natural thing happening."[184]

I wanted the universities to award more honorary doctorates and professorships to jazz artists. To that end, I mailed over one hundred letters and proposals to colleges across the country. I was disappointed that only a few replied.

I gave workshops at the State University of New York at Stony Brook and Hempstead High School under the auspices of the International Art of Jazz. I used Ray Brown's bass method book as a textual reference. I wanted the program directors to stress improvisation studies above reading big band charts.

I told drummer Tony Reedus that dancing would help synchronize his body with rhythm and improve his timekeeping ability. I gave George Coleman Jr. tips on tuning the drums and controlling the bass drum volume. Drummer George Coleman Jr. recalls, "He told me to bring only a hi-hat, snare, and cymbal. We played duets, and he taught me how to swing a rhythm section. I learned much from him."[185]

JAM SESSIONS

The jam session represents an experimental laboratory wherein one can make mistakes and take risks. As young musicians in New York, we had sessions that lasted two and three days. Musicians would have intense debates over correct chord changes, and a cat everyone respected would settle the argument.

We didn't learn to play from gigs alone. As young artists in a competitive environment, we had to develop a unique sound and concept. Today, it's difficult to distinguish one artist from the other. However, in those days, you could identify an artist upon hearing three notes.

It doesn't make sense to grope aimlessly for the basics, so I encouraged my students to seek private instruction to learn proper technique. Many young bassists don't understand . . . the fingers, not amplifiers, produce a great bass sound. I spent many hours playing long tones with the bow; people would be banging on pipes and hitting the ceiling with brooms. In addition, I advised my bass students to tap their feet because standing flat-footed isn't conducive for swinging. And I told them how drug addiction and ignorance of the music business has undermined many potentially brilliant careers and how a sober mind facilitates learning.

Many vocalists in the New York City area attended our "Jazz Discovery" workshops conducted at the Jazz Center of New York. The house rhythm section consisted of Harold Mabern on piano, Frank Gant on drums, and me on bass. We stressed the importance of listening to great vocalists, knowing the key of your song, counting off the correct tempo, no scatting, and basic keyboard knowledge. I taught my students that hollering isn't singing and four beats to the bar ain't swinging. Moreover, we stressed the seriousness and sanctity of the bandstand. The music isn't a game but a well-respected art form.

Lee Willhite was a product of our workshop. After hearing Lee, I was so impressed that I decided to produce his first recording entitled *First Venture*. The independently produced record lacked proper distribution and airplay.

Journalist, William Brower: "First Venture is a welcome event if for no other reason than new male jazz vocalists are rare indeed these days. As jazz vocalists go, Mr. Willhite is a fairly conventional stylist—concentrating on delivery and phrasing of the lyric rather than scat, vocalese or melodic invention. Supporting Willhite is the big-league quartet of Harold Mabern on piano; Jamil Nasser on bass; Frank Gant on drums; and George Coleman on alto saxophone. Coleman, who rarely records on the alto, is impressive both as the principal soloist and as an accompanist."[186]

JAZZ IN THE 80S

The following article details my assessment of jazz in 1984:

The biggest tragedy of all, Nasser says, is that the music cannot survive when its best practitioners are ignored. He thinks trumpeter Wynton Marsalis offers a ray of hope. But one ray isn't enough.[187]

Today, straight ahead jazz players are dismissed as traditionalists or nostalgics while the latest fad of combining jazz with funk, rock, Indian, classical, or electric music is heralded as the true path, the modern counterpart to bebop in the forties. Nasser says that isn't so. He says that bebop's counterpoint in the eighties is still bebop. 'Duke Ellington put it perfectly,' he explains. 'He said it don't mean a thing if it ain't got that swing, makes no difference whether it's cool or hot. Now, we're talkin' about jazz. We're not talkin' about Chinese music. We're not talkin' about Swahili music. We're not talkin' Scandinavian music. We're talkin' about jazz. That's the ballpark. You can't go out and move first base out between third and second and still have a baseball game. Somewhere it has to stay within the boundaries."

The role of improvisation in jazz has been widely misconstrued, both by listeners and musicians, Nasser says. The ultimate goal of jazz isn't experimentation or change, he says, it's to transform the music into a sincere personal statement. If that goal is strived for, innovation will come about naturally. "That's what it's supposed to be," he says. "Take it [the song] and give it your own treatment and let's see how brilliant you can be with this! Let's see how beautiful you can play this piece of music. Let's see if you can take this composition by this particular composer and make it like you wrote it!"

Nasser says that kind of depth is missing from most contemporary jazz. He blames a music industry that has made heroes out of mediocre players, and he also faults the schools.

"I think the universities have crippled these past couple of generations of players because they turned the learning of jazz over to schools with totally unqualified people at the head of them," Nasser claims. "A child came up to [pianist] Harold Mabern and me one night." He recalls, "We were working at the Village Gate as a duo. 'I am terrified,' [the child] told us. We said, 'What are you talkin' about?' He said, 'I just got out of college this year and I just heard you play all those songs, and I don't even know how to begin to think in those terms. Because our jazz teacher . . . all we learned was, he stood us in a circle and he'd say, when I point to you, play whatever comes into your mind, and that's jazz.'

Nasser sneers into his coffee. 'Now how in the world can an institution of higher learning not know this man is 'bullshittin'?' Formalized jazz instruction, says Nasser, places too much emphasis on the mechanics of playing at the expense of studying the masters and developing judgment.

Nasser benefited from both a formal music education and from plenty of years picking the brains of the players he calls "the kings of jazz."

There's no incentive for younger players to strive for greatness when they see the best shuffling to make a living. Or worse, they never even get a chance to hear the best. Today, Nasser is fighting back. Last summer [1984], he produced a series of concerts at the Universal Jazz Coalition's Jazz Center of New York in tribute to the late pianist Red Garland. The concerts were held at the same time as the KOOL New York Jazz Festival. KOOL didn't have time to include Nasser or guitarist Chuck Wayne, Phineas Newborn Jr., trumpeter Bill Hardman or saxophonists George Coleman, Lou Donaldson, Harold Vick, and Clifford Jordan. So, the musicians put on their own festival.

"At The Jazz Center in New York, we came together, pooling our talents to give the people an idea of what the full doses are," Nasser says. "But we also have to get the full doses out in places like this—Arizona and New Mexico. Because I think, personally, that this is where we can re-incubate the art in the proper way.

"It's time to correct these things, but we don't have a lot of time," Nasser says. "We don't have time, and when we see our kings, who were so important to this movement . . . leaving without talking . . . we don't have time." He runs his spoon through his coffee slowly.

"Some people think that I'm being an alarmist," he says. "But see, I went through the rhythm and blues genocide. I was there. Now I'm lookin' at the jazz genocide and I'm gonna holler long and loud on this one."[188]

FREE JAZZ VS STRAIGHT AHEAD JAZZ

This field of classical jazz began with Louis Armstrong and everything underneath can be likened unto the fire that cooks the roast. Mr. Armstrong was the roast. Jazz history has continuity. You can hear traces of Louis Armstrong in Roy Eldridge and Dizzy Gillespie. Each generation builds upon the foundation of their predecessors.

Then a group of musicians attempted to disregard the traditional concepts and ideas. They called the music "free jazz." I remember reading about an art experiment wherein they allowed chimpanzees to paint then put expensive frames around what they created. The art critics, so-called experts, lauded their brilliant brushstrokes.

The avant-garde community is fraught with frauds, who couldn't play and didn't have the talent or knowledge. Thus, we wouldn't allow them on the bandstand. For example, alto saxophonist, Marion Brown, had to check his horn at the door before entering Birdland. The 'free jazz' movement, however, provided a loophole for him and others to work as jazz artists.

I issued the following challenge to them. Let us go before a Harlem audience, let the straight-ahead artists play out, and the avant-garde musicians play straight ahead—then let the audience decide who the real masters are. Avant-garde pushed many of our African American listeners over to Motown and James Brown. If our people can't dance or at least tap their feet to the music—they're out of there. I remember Stan Getz played at the Blue Coronet in Brooklyn, and the players and hustlers who brought their dates wanted to hear "Desafinado." But Getz played free jazz and one of those dangerous hustlers said, "Get that motherfucker out of here." The manager canceled the gig.

One exception that comes to mind is Pharoah Sanders. I loved the way he skillfully fused controlled avant-garde with straight-ahead jazz in his great original compositions. He loved having me and Idris Muhammad in the rhythm section, because we could turn those corners with him.

Jim Mason reviewed our 1980 performance at Virginia Commonwealth University in Richmond, VA, "As a unit, the quartet members played with clarity and a keen interplay among their instruments — John Hicks piano, Jameel [sic] Nasser's upright bass and Idris Muhammad's forceful but tasteful drumming. Together, they provided a fine aural backdrop for Sanders' solo flights."[189]

I played a duo gig at Slugs with McCoy Tyner, and we played free: no music, no tonal center, or fixed tempo. I felt so uncomfortable; I asked him for a sketch. But, he said, "What you're playing is fine." I prefer to play with a sense of direction and structure.

Speaking of freedom, jazz musicians had a freedom struggle that predated and eventually ran parallel to the 1960s Civil Rights Movement.

15

JAZZ AND JUSTICE

*Black musicians greatly mistrusted the union, and most
jazz musicians saw the union as an enforcer of rules rather
than as an ally at work. The union was long overdue in
doing something for the jazz artists. When John Gensel
became president, I met with him during a snowstorm on his
first day in office, and I pressed Gensel to be in brotherhood
with the jazz musicians.*

—JAMIL NASSER

*D*r. *Martin Luther King Jr: "Jazz speaks of life. Blues tells a story of
life's difficulty, and if you think for a moment, you will realize they
take the hardest realities of life and put them into music, only to come out
with some new hope or sense of triumph. Much of our power in the freedom
movement in the United States has come from the music. It has strength-
ened us with its sweet rhythms when courage began to fall. It has calmed us
with its rich harmonies when spirits were down."* [190]
What does Jazz and Justice mean? Papa Jo Jones answered
the question when he said, "A representative from the Student
Nonviolent Coordinating Committee came backstage to ask Ella

Fitzgerald to join a civil rights march, but I interceded to answer for her, Get the fuck outta here, she's been marching!"[191]

Ella and many musicians of their generation and before challenged racism in the Deep South and elsewhere in the '30s and '40s. Our revolution was a quiet one as it lacked the collective organization and mobilization to dramatize its agenda. It was led by courageous individuals and organizations, who resented the plantation like nature of the jazz business and desired to own their music. I know my willingness to speak out against racism in jazz circumscribed my career as well as several artists cited in this chapter: Lucky Thompson, Hazel Scott, and Abbey Lincoln.

The following article "Jazzocide" contains my assessment of the 1984 jazz industry: Jazz is dying. The cause of death will be attributed to old age, but there are signs of foul play. The culprits are many—a music industry that systematically restricts black access, an educational system staffed by incompetents, musicians who seem to have no understanding of the most important values in jazz, and a public that has been misled, misinformed, and confused to the point that it doesn't know what jazz is.

'The music industry is bent on excluding blacks from reaping their just rewards from an art form they created.' The root cause of the problem, he says, is racism: 'Its cliques, plantations, and special interests,' Nasser says, 'and it's sophisticated now. It's not so overt as to call attention to itself, but it's very bad for us. When you look around and see great black artists . . . with no record contract, and who haven't had one in a long time. But on the other side, on the white side, you can have lots of greats, and even the mediocre can soon get into the arena.'

Besides playing with Newborn's trio through 1958, Nasser also played and recorded with such figures as Lou Donaldson, John Coltrane, and Randy Weston. During those days, he says, relations between black and white players were the best they've ever been. Today, he says, those relations are strained.

"It's crescendo and decrescendo," he remarks. "When it was in crescendo, it was when the white artists were out with us, hanging out, learning, sharing this, and sharing that. That was us opening up, saying 'welcome.' And now it's in decrescendo because those same people are the ones who are being put up as the kings, and in my opinion, for them to be silent, is to acquiesce to what's going on. I don't think we'd allow them to be buried. I wouldn't have allowed an Al Haig to be buried. I wouldn't have tolerated that because Al Haig was an artist. Charlie Parker hired Al Haig."

Eli "Lucky" Thompson was a great tenor saxophonist and composer. In 1947, he recorded with Charlie Parker on the legendary Dial Sessions in Los Angeles and performed with Parker and Gillespie at Billy Berg's. In addition, Lucky played rhythm and blues sessions around the country. I would encourage the reader to listen to the Miles Davis recording *Walkin* as well as *Lucky Strikes*. These sessions exemplify his brilliance. What should have been a promising career came to a screeching halt, because Lucky demanded respect and self-ownership.

He established a publishing company called Great Music in 1949. Lucky's friend and associate, Hank Jones, said: *"Some people might say that the powers that be resented the fact that he had the temerity to have his own publishing company. Lucky didn't have the type of personality that would sit back and accept anything anyone wanted to hand out. The publishing situation is grand theft . . . it's thievery of the highest order . . . I'm sure this has a lot to do with Lucky's attitude—if you want to call it that. It is a normal reaction that any sane intelligent person would have if someone has been taking advantage of you all your life."[192]*

He expressed the following gripes with jazz industry: "Hastily thrown together sessions (concerts or recordings) which allows the musicians no time to build up a group feeling. A manager or club owners that tell you whom you should hire for your band and recording officials that tell you how you should play. These vultures will do anything to tie you up, even pay you double money to bait the trap. When they have you, they tell you what to do, what to play, and what to say, maybe. If you buck them over anything, they'll leave you on the shelf. Yes, they try to starve you. You have to take a beating for what you believe." [193]

In 1956, Lucky flew to Paris for a series of engagements. He had a fear of flying and therefore wanted to exit the plane as soon as possible. But Joe Glaser, the President of Associated Booking and Louis Armstrong's manager, wanted Louis to exit first. He ordered Lucky not to exit the plane before Louis. When Thompson refused to obey, Glaser said, "You're finished in this country and all over the world." An industrywide boycott of Lucky Thompson followed Glaser's statement.

Lucky Thompson: "There is no heart any more. This is a cold and calculating business. A few like me are a thorn in the side to those who run things." [194]

"Jazz is acknowledged to be America's greatest contribution to the field of music. But now it has been reduced to a kind of fad, with one fad after another, taking the place of healthy inspiring beautiful art. These fads are better known as the modern, west coast, and cool school. This desperate attempt of many critics—supported by booking agents, publishers, and recording companies—to inject a form of white supremacy in jazz is partly the reason for the fad." [195]

Lucky Thompson expired on July 30, 2005; he was eighty-one years old. Mr. Thompson was a leader in the quest for African-American ownership, respect, and freedom in the jazz business.

I worked with two talented, African American woman artists, who paid heavy dues for their political views and activism, Hazel Scott and Abbey Lincoln. I told a journalist, "She's everything I thought she would be and more. Hazel is one of our queens. She is an original; a genius who defies category. But we as a people do not rally to our performers who are geniuses now. Our people are led away by Madison Avenue, which often picks mediocre talent to constantly expose and promote." [196]

"She protested against the arbitrary listing of performers who were alleged to be left-wing or Communist sympathizers, including herself, in Red Channels. Anyone listed in the book would be automatically barred or

dismissed from theatrical and television jobs without the benefit of a defense or rebuttal. Hazel said, "The tag on those performers listed covers them with the filth of scandal and mud of besmirched reputations. We should not be written off by the vicious slanders and unverified charges of petty men." Hazel's solution? "Unions and performers should boycott networks and sponsors who suspend entertainers without proof."

One arrogant Congressman had the temerity to tell Hazel, "We have agreed to hear you because you are the wife of our colleague." She replied, "Well, what about the 400 entertainers who are not? I responded. Yes, I had appeared at many benefits for just causes. I'd do it again. That upset them. The whole thing taught me never to get involved in international, national, or local politics. They're all filthy!" [197] Scarce work prospects in America forced Hazel Scott into exile: She lived and worked in Paris for three years.

Abbey Lincoln excelled as an actress, vocalist, songwriter, visual artist, clothing designer, and political activist. Abbey's singing on *We Insist! Freedom Now*, and her outspoken views on racism didn't increase her commercial viability. After Patrice Lumumba's assassination, she was among protesters brutalized by New York City police officers at the United Nations.

Abbey made the following statements during a panel discussion on racism and jazz: *"And they did Gene Krupa's life story, and Jo Jones is still eating grits." "The reason we don't get in is because—we may be the greatest ever—we are not allowed in because of our dark faces. Is that not true?" "The black man is so eager to integrate it makes me sick. He's eager for anything he can integrate into. It's the white man who doesn't want to integrate. Do I want to Integrate? Not necessarily. Integrate into what? Why do I necessarily have to want to integrate? I have been refused all this time. Maybe I have decided, I like being with my own people. Do you believe you have the right to tell me, I must integrate with people who have always abused me and looked at me askance?"* [198] In 1972, following a trip to Africa, Abbey changed in her name to Aminata Moseka.

In 1984, I scheduled a meeting with Reverend Jesse Jackson, who made his first presidential bid that year. During our phone conversation, he expressed interest in my ideas for expanding the jazz audience. I flew to his campaign office in Washington DC. I wanted him to mention the plight of Lucky Thompson and the Kings Series' mission to preserve our music. This kind of publicity would have afforded me more influence. But he said, "Before we get started, remember, I'm not a politician: I'm a man of God." His statement summarily ended our meeting. What a disappointment! The presidency is not a religious office.

I had two interviews with Gil Noble, the journalist and host of *Like It Is*. One day, I went to his office and found him under emotional duress.

"They're trying to take my show," he said.

"Why?" I asked.

"I had a show that gave the Palestinian perspective on the Israeli conflict and made some enemies in the process."

I said, "You can't fight alone. Call Amiri Baraka, Harry Belafonte, and Jesse Jackson and tell them to have their friends and associates to call and write letters." Everyone delivered and *Like It Is* escaped the chopping block.

I hope jazz musicians appreciate the sacrifices that me, Lucky Thompson, Abbey Lincoln, Hazel Scott, Gigi Gryce, and others made to rectify the injustices in the jazz industry. Many musicians wouldn't remotely consider speaking truth to power or leading a movement against the jazz plantation.

16

FAMILY PORTRAIT

I wouldn't consider marriage and family before I traveled the
world and had a firm foothold in my career. Consequently, I
practiced and developed my music without short changing
a family of the love and attention they need to thrive.

—JAMIL NASSER

As I stated in the preface, my father wanted to document his musical experiences. But fatherhood is an essential part of his legacy. Although I will not discuss the inner dynamics of his relationships, my father was married three times. His first wife was Pat; second Karimah; and third Baano. Karimah gave birth to four children: Umar was born on July 20, 1964; Aliyah on August 25, 1965; Muneer on June 3, 1967; and Zaid on September 16, 1968. Baano birthed one child, Najee, on May 3, 1981.

FLASHBACKS
I remember watching Dad change a flat tire (circa 1972) on his black Cadillac. Then the jack came loose and the tire rim collapsed on his finger. With sheer terror on his face, he ran inside and placed his profusely bleeding finger under the bathroom sink. When I asked him about that day, he said, "I thought my bass playing days were over, because

it opened up a deep gash on my right index finger." We lived on 293 Central Park West, near the Museum of Natural History, and Dad would often take us across the street to the park. He recalled, "One day, I took you (Muneer), Aliyah, and Umar to the park on a beautiful, sunny day. It was jam packed. I turned my back for what seemed like a few seconds, and you were gone. My heart pounded as I frantically searched the playground. I sat Umar and Aliyah on a park bench and told them to stay there. Finally, I saw, off in the distance, a faint image of a little boy between two men. I ran down the street, grabbed your hand, and said, "Where are you going with my son?" I was so angry that I can't remember what they said. Boy, I never spanked you like I did on that day, but it curbed your wandering tendencies."

I taught my children the alphabet, basic reading, and math. When Aliyah's first grade teacher claimed, she had a learning disability, I quizzed her before the teacher on the concepts that supposedly eluded her grasp. She nailed every question, and the teacher was astounded. I told her, "The problem is yours not my daughter's." Umar was so perceptive; I taught him how to ride the buses and subways. One day, his aunt was running a high fever and desperately needed prescription medication. So, she gave Umar—only six years old—precise directions to the pharmacy and paced the floor waiting for him. To her surprise and relief, he returned with the medicine.

One day a man living in our building gave my sister and me, socks filled with pennies. And we ran back brimming with excitement to show Dad, but he took us back and made us return the money. Years later, I asked him why and he said, "Child molesters use gifts as bait for potential victims."

Dad recalled, "Karimah, like many women at that time, had the Dr. Spock book on child rearing which contained some strange concepts like permissive parenting which included not spanking kids and tolerating temper tantrums etc. I happen to disagree with many of them . . . we argued over this book, so finally, I threw it out the window."

In 1973, mom and dad had a violent confrontation, which resulted in ripped clothing, cuts and abrasions, and four crying children. They

separated shortly after this fight; however, Dad maintained an active pres-
ence in our lives. We remained on Long Island, and he moved back to New
York City.

OUR FATHER

Dad emphasized spirituality, moral discipline, and education. He
read the Qur'an to us and took us to the mosque for Eid celebra-
tions (the Muslim holiday after Ramadan). And the recitation of
the Al-Fatiha (opening chapter of the Qur'an) preceded each meal.

In addition, he gave us a guided tour of junkie habitat in the
east village (Bowery). The junkies nodding off on corners amused
us. He said, "I rather see you dead than a slave to dope." It worked
because none of us became drug addicts. Dad encouraged us to ask
him about drugs, because he had sampled many of them. While
he supported our participation in music, academic achievement
took precedence over all other pursuits. "Transcend mediocrity,
be a leader, and don't be a musical dummy," he said. If we brought
home sub-standard grades, a meeting with our teachers soon followed. Moreover, hanging out with friends and other activities
were suspended until our grades improved.

The Hempstead Public School System had both high achievers
and thugs—some went to Yale and others went to jail. Marijuana
and alcohol were as present as books and teachers. And the possi-
bility of sexual contact loomed large. Dad told us, "If you produce
a child, then you must move out and get a job."

He attended most of our concerts, school plays, and award
ceremonies. We earnestly looked forward to his weekend visits.
Our activities spanned the gamut: fishing, roller-skating, jazz concerts, holiday parades, movies, amusement parks, carnivals, museums, and Broadway plays et al. Dad always told us to ask questions
about anything, because he interacted with people in the streets
and the suites.

Dad taught us by precept and example to stand up for our beliefs. As Muslim children growing up in the seventies, we were subject to mockery from schoolmates and teachers. On a few occasions, he had to excoriate teachers who made ignorant statements about Islam. When Dad took to the airwaves to discuss racism or other controversial topics, his workload suffered. Thus, we braved some difficult days fraught with hunger and deprivation. Nevertheless, we supported him one hundred percent.

He read several newspapers daily and completed the crossword puzzles. And Dad maintained an archive of articles on various subject matters, and we often discussed and debated international and national political issues. Never content just to play music, Dad placed a high premium on political and social awareness. And he resented Uncle Tom, African Americans who refused to take a stand against racism and injustice.

He sent us to Memphis during summer breaks to meet our grandparents, aunts, uncles, and cousins. So, we learned about Memphis culture and his early life. Although my grandparents respected our dietary restrictions, church and Sunday school attendance were mandatory. Our visits to Memphis were an outgrowth of his love and respect for family. In short, Jamil Nasser was a serious father who successfully and lovingly fulfilled his obligations as such.

HAJJ TO MECCA

Umar Nasser: In 2001, Dad arrived in Jeddah, Saudi Arabia. The group coordinator searched for him—ten hours later—he finally reached Mecca. After greeting me, Dad requested coffee and fresh figs. I purchased fresh figs and Nescafe instant coffee. He shook his head at the Nescafe and said, "That's not real coffee." I went back and purchased a Mr. Coffee machine and Maxwell House coffee; he appreciated the upgrade. Dad is usually talkative and inquisitive; but on this occasion, he was reticent. In retrospect, I realize this behavioral change must have been the early stages of Alzheimer's.

Most of the Hajj groups traveled by bus to different Hajj ritual sites, and the traffic congestion prolongs the travel time. For example, destinations accessible in forty-five minutes on foot would take four to five hours by bus, so we walked to the Hajj ritual sites. We had a tent location in Mina and an apartment outside of Mina. The apartment served as a rest stop for dad to have coffee and a nap.

The first time we entered Masjid Al Haram in Mecca, I closely observed Dad to see his response upon viewing the Kaaba. Surprisingly, he remained quite stoic. After the Tawaf (the circumambulation seven times of the Holy Kaaba), we completed Isha prayer, looked down on the Kaaba, and then Dad's tears started to flow.

We attended a Janaza (funeral prayer), and the imam made one Taslim (the portion of Islamic prayer when the worshipper recites Salaam Alaikum once facing to the right and once facing to the left). Speaking for the first since we entered Masjid Al Haram, he said, "I never saw that, but I like it." I later told the imam who conducted Dad's funeral to make one Taslim to the right. After completing, the Meccan portion of Hajj, we went to Masjid Nawabi (the Prophet's Mosque) in Medina. We stayed for two days and headed back to the Jeddah airport for his departure. Many people who remembered us walking during Hajj asked, "How is your father?"

Once back the United States, he called every week to confirm US new reports about Saudi Arabia. He said, "You got it, boy; you got it." I asked him what he meant and he said, "You got Islam."[199]

ZAID NASSER

It's 1:00 a.m. at Smalls, an intimate jazz club in Greenwich Village; a brilliant, young alto saxophonist has concluded a great set and is walking through the audience. A beautiful lady stepped in his path and said, "I

*came specifically to hear you . . . are you going to play another set?" He
replied, "No, but I will be here tomorrow." She said, "Okay, I'll come back."
The woman was the great actress, Lynn Whitfield, and the alto saxophonist, Zaid Nasser.*

Zaid began playing clarinet in 1975; four years later, he auditioned for the International Art of Jazz workshop at Hempstead
High School. And tenor saxophonist Bill Saxton, who was the
band director and the saxophone instructor, accepted him despite
his young age (eleven years old). As a junior high school student,
he performed with the Hempstead High School Pit Orchestra and
Jazz Ensemble. After playing clarinet for nine years, Zaid transi-
tioned to alto saxophone. As a precocious young student, with an
acute ear, he transcribed solos by Charlie Parker, Lou Donaldson,
Cannonball Adderley, and George Coleman.

Dad told George Coleman about Zaid's budding talent, so
George invited Zaid to play a set with him. Coleman called an up-
tempo blues, which segued into an extended blues sermon that
ended with a fiery set of passages . . . then Zaid emerged from the
shadows and played his ass off. Dad said, "Zaid surprised me coming out on the racehorse number. I harbored an element of doubt,
but after the first chorus . . . he dispelled any doubts."

Under the tutelage of Coleman, Zaid began to soar. George
taught me, "There's nothing worse than an ignorant musician. You
must master your instrument and the science of creating music."
Furthermore, he encouraged me to find my own style rather than
just imitating other great saxophonists. I remember going for a
lesson with him and he said, "You're bullshitting, go practice, and
come back when you have it together." For those who wonder
about the difficulty level of George's bandstand—Dad always challenged cocky musicians who thought they had their shit together
to join them—it was rough. Mr. Coleman's musical menu included:
fast tempos, random time and key changes, two-fives descending
chromatically, in whole steps, thirds, fourths—the works. I made it
through, but it was no joke."[200]

New York City in the '80s offered a young musician a chance to hear and perform with the masters, and he took full advantage of this environment performing with Lou Donaldson, Junior Cook, Frank Foster, Cecil Payne, Ron Carter, Clifford Jordan, C. Sharpe, Tommy Turrentine, and many others. One night, Zaid walked from Washington Heights in New York City to Englewood, NJ, after playing two sets with Lou Donaldson.

After graduating from Dwight Morrow High School, he attended Howard University for a semester, then went to Memphis, where he performed with the legendary Roselle Claxton, Phineas and Calvin Newborn, Gerald Wilson, and Herman Green. In 1989, he left Memphis and moved to New York City. Zaid played consistently at Smalls throughout the 1990s. On several occasions, he hired Jamil Nasser, Frank Gant, Billy Kaye, and Jimmy Lovelace. His recording *Live at Smalls* documents this period. Listen to the mature command he displays on the ballad "Everything happens to me."

In 1990, Art Blakey asked Zaid to audition for the Jazz Messengers at Sweet Basil; unfortunately, Mr. Blakey was too ill to complete the engagement and expired a few months later. When New York gigs dwindled—determined to pursue music on a full-time basis—he set sailed on the Carnival Cruise line traveling throughout the Caribbean and Mexico. His original composition "Escape from New York" speaks to this phase of his development. Music has taken Zaid to Russia, Turkey, Armenia, Dubai, and many other places. Zaid and Dad appear on Ned Otter's recording *Secrets Inside* as well as private recordings at Smalls. Zaid continues to spread joy and happiness around the world drawing upon the historical foundation laid out by our father and other musical giants.

17

MEMORIAL REVIEW

On March 21, 2010, at St. Peter's Church family, friends, and musical associates gathered to pay tribute to Jamil Nasser, the great bassist, composer, historian, and concert promoter who passed on to ancestry on February 13, 2010. Jamil left a legacy on multiple levels. He recorded and performed with artists such as Ahmad Jamal, John Coltrane, Lou Donaldson, Booker Little, Phineas Newborn, George Coleman, Randy Weston, Al Haig, Harold Mabern, Monty Alexander, Gene Ammons, Sonny Stitt, Kenny Dorham, Hank Mobley, Donald Byrd, B.B. King, Johnny Ace, Hazel Scott, Dorothy Donegan, and many more. He was the vice president of the Jazz Foundation of America and an educator, who conducted no-nonsense, jazz workshops and performances under the auspices of the Universal Jazz Coalition. Cobi Narita, Founder and Director of the Universal Jazz Coalition, a close friend and associate of Jamil's, organized the memorial.

Harold Mabern kicked off the memorial with a spirited solo rendition of his original composition "Rakin and Scrapin." Harold said, "Jamil was a giver, not a taker, a man of high integrity, and an organizer who didn't waste time." His long-time friend and associate Frank Gant, using a miniature xylophone, performed a duet with Frank Owens on "Amazing Grace."

I read a statement by Ahmad Jamal: "The gift of mutual friendship and trust between Jamil and I will take volumes to put into words. In short, he and I explored many avenues together musically, philosophically, family-wise, business-wise, and on and on. Our spiritual development and pursuits took us all over the world. He has left a grand legacy and that will be thought about and prayed about by all his friends and family members throughout their lives." Accompanied by Harold Mabern, Lyle Atkinson, and Carl Allen, I performed an upbeat "Song for My Father" on flugelhorn.

Next, saxophonist and composer Jimmy Heath, accompanied by Barry Harris on piano, played a beautiful rendition of "There Will Never Be Another You." Monty Alexander performed a heartfelt interpretation of Jamil's "Tropical Breeze" and segued into the Bob Marley classic "No Woman No Cry." Randy Weston began by mentioning two special recordings he made with Jamil, *Little Niles* and *Evening with the Boston Pops*. He said, "Jamil introduced me to three giants of the jazz piano: Ahmad Jamal, Oscar Dennard, and Phineas Newborn." Randy accompanied by Alex Blake on bass and Benny Powell on trombone played a riveting version of "Blue Moses."

Vocalist Carline Ray sang a haunting version of "Everything Must Change." The great pianist Norman Simmons and Lyle Atkinson performed a beautiful and thematic rendition of "If I Should Lose You." Lou Donaldson said, "Jamil and I talked every day. He worked night and day to implement the heath care program for musicians at Englewood Hospital and drove some of the musicians to the hospital."

Lou performed a classic version of the standard "Body and Soul," his rhythm section consisting of Richard Wyands on piano, Michael Fleming on bass, and Jackie Williams on drums. Fellow Memphian and tenor saxophonist, George Coleman, along with his student Ned Otter on tenor, Mike LaDonne on piano, Lyle Atkinson on bass, and George Coleman Jr. on drums; performed a fantastic version of "I'll Be Seeing You." The great tenor saxophonist, flautist, and arranger Frank Wess opened with a graceful solo rendition of "The Summer Knows." He was joined by Richard Wyands on piano, Michael Fleming on bass, and Ray Mosca on drums on a swinging version of "I Remember You."

Trumpeter Jimmy Owens, who worked alongside Jamil in the Jazz Foundation and on the Jazz Advisory Committee to Local 802, reminded the audience of Jamil's role in establishing the Jazz Emergency Fund. Moreover, Jimmy mentioned that Jamil addressed the U.S. House of Representatives to influence the passing of House Resolution HR-57, a bill introduced by Congressman John Conyers (D-Mich) that declared jazz to be a national treasure.

Then Jimmy picked up his flugelhorn and played a wonderful blues solo with a majestic tone. Jamil's wife, Baano Nasser, thanked Cobi Narita for organizing the tribute, the legendary musicians for participating, and family/friends for their support. Jamil's sister Dorothy Robinson and his granddaughter Yasmin Nasser read an honorary proclamation from the Mayor of Memphis, Joe Ford. The tribute concluded with a jam session led by Monty Alexander with Michael Fleming on bass and Wade Barnes on drums playing a house rocking blues. Frank Owens took over the piano, Dotti Taylor, flautist and president of International Woman in Jazz, and Muneer on trumpet closed with "Straight No Chaser" by Thelonious Monk. Jamil Nasser's tribute at St. Peter's Church was a first-class event for one of the greatest musicians and human beings to walk the earth. The memorial reflected his stature and influence in the jazz community and the world in general. Long Live Jamil Nasser!

CHRONOLOGICAL DISCOGRAPHY OF JAMIL NASSER

1. Phineas Newborn Duke Peacock Records, 1953 recorded "Round Midnight" and "How High the Moon" two 78 tracks (Jazz 500)
2. Johnny Ace *Cross My Heart* Duke Peacock Records, 1953
3. Phineas Newborn *Phineas Rainbow* RCA Victor, October 16, 1956 (RCA Victor LPM 1421)
4. Phineas Newborn *While My Lady Sleeps* RCA Victor, April 23–24, 1957(RCA Victor LPM 1474)
5. Hank Mobley *Curtain Call*Bluenote, August 18, 1957 (BLI 61006)
6. Red Garland *Soul Junction* Prestige, November 15, 1957 (PRLP 7181)
7. Red Garland *All Mornin Long* Prestige, November 15, 1957 (PRLP 7130)
8. Red Garland *High Pressure* Prestige, December 13, 1957 (PRLP 7209)
9. Red Garland *Dig It* Prestige, December 13, 1957 (PRLP 7729)
10. Lou Donaldson *Lou Takes Off* Bluenote, December 15, 1957 (BLP 1591)
11. Gene Ammons *The Big Sound* Prestige, January 3, 1958 (PRLP 7201)
12. Gene Ammons *Groove Blues* Prestige, January 3, 1958 (PRLP 7201)
13. Herbie Mann *Just Wailin* Prestige, February 14, 1958 (NJ-8211)
14. Phineas Newborn *Fabulous Phineas* RCA Victor, March 28, 1958 (LPM 1873)
15. Evans Bradshaw *Look Out* Riverside, June 9, 1958 (RLP 12-263)
16. Randy Weston *New Faces at Newport* July 5, 1958 (MetroJazz E1005) (MM2085) (LP)

17. Red Garland *Rojo* Prestige, August 22, 1958 (PRLP 7198)
18. Randy Weston *Little Niles* United Artists, October 1958 (UAL 4011/5011)
19. Melba Liston *Melba and Her Bones* Prestige, December 28, 1958 (MetroJazz SE1013)
20. Lionel Hampton *Golden Vibes* RCA Victor, 1959 (CS 8110)
21. Memphis Musicians *Down Home Reunion* United Artists, 1959 (UA 59544)
22. Lester Young *Lester Young in Paris* Verve, March 4, 1959 (MGV 8378)
23. Oscar Dennard *Legendary Oscar Dennard* Something Else Classic, April 1959
24. Flavio Ambrosetti *Anniversary* Enja, 1961
25. Buddy Collette *Modern Jazz* v.5 (Milan, Italy) Stella, March 1961 (LPS 6108)
26. Eric Dolphy *Berlin Concerts* Enja, August 30, 1961 (Enja 3017)
27. Franco Cerri *International Jazz Meeting* (Milan, Italy) 1961 (DIW 3022)
28. George Joyner *George Joyner* (Milan, Italy), 1961
29. Lillian Terry *The Four of Us*, December 1961 (CGD-N 9334)
30. George Gruntz *Don't Mean a Thing* (Lugano, Switzerland), January 1962 (ENJ-9027-2)
31. Ahmad Jamal *Naked City Theme* Cadet, June 26-28, 1964 (DJLP-733)
32. Ahmad Jamal *Roar of the Greasepaint Smell of the Crowd* Cadet, Argo, February 24-25, 1965 (LPS-751)
33. Ahmad Jamal *Extensions* Argo, May 18-20, 1965 (LPS-758)
34. Ahmad Jamal *Rhapsody* Cadet, December 15-17, 1966 (LPS-764)
35. Ahmad Jamal *Heatwave* Cadet, February 15-17, 1966 (LPS-777)
36. Ahmad Jamal *Cry Young* Cadet, June 12-13, 1967 (LPS-792)
37. Ahmad Jamal Trio (unissued tracks) July 1967

38. Ahmad Jamal *The Bright, the Blue, and the Beautiful* Cadet, February 12-137, 1968 (LPS-807)
39. Ahmad Jamal *Live at the Top* Impulse, 1968 (AS 9176)
40. Ahmad Jamal *Tranquility* Impulse, 1968 (ABCS-660)
41. Ahmad Jamal *The Awakening* MCA, February 2-3, 1970 (MCA-5644)
42. Ahmad Jamal *Freeflight Live at Montreux* Impulse, July 17, 1971 (RM-1993)
43. Ahmad Jamal *Outerspaceinnertime* (Montreux, Switzerland) Impulse, July 17, 1971 (AS-9226)
44. Ahmad Jamal *Jamalca* 20th Century Fox Records, 1973 (T-432)
45. Ahmad Jamal *Plays Jamal* 20th Century Fox Records, 1974 (T-459)
46. Ahmad Jamal *Live at the Jazz Workshop*, March 30, 1974 (private recording)
47. Ahmad Jamal *Live at the Jazz Workshop*, May 23, 1974 (private recording)
48. Ahmad Jamal *Genetic Walk* 20th Century Fox Records, 1975 (T-600)
49. Al Haig *Strings Attached* Choice, March 27, 1975 (CRS-1010)
50. Al Haig *Interplay* Venus, November 6, 1976 (SB-1005)
51. Al Haig *Serendipity* Century, February 19, 1977 (CECC-00281)
52. Al Haig *Portrait of Bud Powell* Absorb Music Japan, July 11, 1977 (ABCJ66)
53. Al Haig *Ornithology* Progressive, July 22, 1977 (PCD-7024)
54. Al Haig *Enigma* Jazz Ball Records, November 2, 1977
55. Al Haig *I Remember Bebop* Columbia, November 5, 1977 (C2-36381)
56. Louis Smith *Just Friends* Steeplechase, March 19, 1978 (532449)

57. Cybill Shepherd *Vanilla* Gold Castle, August 1978 (GC-76543)

58. Al Haig *Expressly Ellington* Spotlite October 14, 1978 (E) (SPJ 20)

59. Al Haig *Un Poco Loco* Spotlite, 1978 (E) (SPJ 701 CD)

60. George Coleman, Harold Vick, Sal Nistico, Frank Wess, and Ricky Ford *Shootout on Eleventh Street,* January 15, 1979 (unreleased)

61. Mari Nakamoto *Something Blue* Zen Label May 14, 1979 London (1011)

62. Harold Mabern *Pisces Calling* Trident, 1980 (TRS-506)

63. Al Haig *Plays the Music of Jerome Kern* Inner City Records, 1980

64. Red Garland *In the Wee Small Hours of the Morning* Fullhouse February 5, 1980 (J) (PAP 9211)

65. Red Garland *Fine and Dandy,* Lobster February 6, 1980 (J FLA 1060)

66. Randy Weston *Three Africans Queen with the Boston Pops Symphony,* 1981 (unreleased)

67. Lee Willhite *First Venture* Tampa Records, October 22, 1981

68. Monty Alexander *Live in Aix-en-Provence,* 1981 (2 tracks)

69. Red Garland *Misty Red* Timeless, April 12-13, 1982 (Du) SJP 179

70. Eddie Heywood *Now* Syn, 1982 (1p 7604)

71. Pharoah Sanders *Live at Sweet Basil* January 15, 1983 (private recording)

72. Monty Alexander, Barry Harris, Walter Bishop Jr, Dick Katz, Harold Mabern, and Cedar Walton *Tribute to Al Haig,* Live at the Village Gate, February 13, 1983 Live at the Village Gate

73. Kay Boyd *First Slice* Spotlight, August 1983

74. *Art Farmer Live at Defemio's,* Art Farmer, Mickey Tucker and Larry Willis, Jamil Nasser, and Al Defemio December 13 and 14, 1984 (private recording)

75. Phineas Newborn *Live at Sweet Basil* May 4, 1984 (private recording)
76. Lou Donaldson, George Coleman, Clifford Jordan, Harold Vick, Phineas Newborn Solo *Tribute to Red Garland,* June 1984
77. George Coleman *Live at Defemio's,* circa 1984 (private recording)
78. Frank Wess Quintet with Kenny Barron and Marvin "Smitty" Smith *Live at the Passaic County Public Library* January 6, 1985
79. George Coleman *Manhattan Panorama* Theresa Records, 1985 (B000KS12UM)
80. Hilton Ruiz *Live at the West End* circa May 1986 (private recording)
81. Adam Markowicz *Moonray* Novus, 1986 (300-1-N)
82. Phineas Newborn with Adam Markowicz (unissued) April 20, 1986
83. Phineas Newborn *I Have Something to Say* Emarcy, November 11-12, 1987 (J) (32JD10148)
84. Jamil Nasser Quintet *Live at the United Nations* November 20, 1987 (unreleased)
85. Jamil Nasser and the Bassoon Choir *Tribute to Israel Crosby, Walter Page, and Oscar Pettiford* Live at Jazz Center of New York, June 6, 1987 (unreleased)
86. Jamil Nasser, Harold Mabern, Junior Cook, Jimmy Heath Frank Wess, Abbey Lincoln, George Coleman, and Frank Gant *Tribute to Harold Vick,* February 1988
87. Randy Weston *Well You Needn't* June 3, 1989 (841 3132 CD)
88. Randy Weston *Portraits of Duke Ellington* Verve, June 4, 1989 (841 3122 CD)
89. Randy Weston *Self Portraits,* June 5, 1989 (Verve 841 3142 CD)

90. Randy Weston *Live in Toronto* 1989 (unreleased radio broadcast)
91. Lewis Keel *Come Out Swinging*, Muse 1990 (5438)
92. Randy Weston *Spirit of Our Ancestors* Verve, May 20-22, 1991 (511 857-2) (2CDs)
93. James Williams *Memphis Convention* DIW, July-August 1992
94. Randy Weston *Volcano Blues* Antilles, 1993 (Verve/Gitanes 519 259-2 CD)
95. Ahmad Jamal *The Essence Part 1* February 8, 1994 Polydor (529 327-2)
96. Ahmad Jamal *Big Byrd* Verve, February 6-7, 1995 (314 533 477-2)
97. George Coleman *I Could Write a Book* Telarc January 8-9, 1998 CD (83439)
98. Calvin Newborn *Upcity* Yellow Dog Records, 1998 (21157)
99. Hideaki Yoshioka *Moment to Moment* Tokuma Japan Comm. 2000 (B00005GGE6)
100. Ahmad Jamal *Perfect Picture* May 20-24, 2000
101. Jazz Foundation *A Great Day in Harlem*, 2002
102. Ned Otter *Secrets Inside Two & Four*, 2002 (Zaid Nasser on Alto) (4)

COMPOSITIONS

1. Clarisse
2. Abu' Beat
3. Moroccan Garden's
4. Bruno's Blues
5. Blue Chains
6. Alexandria
7. Of Bass, I Love with Jamal
8. Apology with Jamal
9. Tropical Breeze
10. Fiddle Fire
11. Big Bad Beale
12. String Fever
13. Minor Mood's lyrics

Notes

1. Ted, Gioia, *The History of Jazz*, second edition (Oxford: Oxford University Press, 2011), 235.

2. Ben Yagoda, *The B Side: The Death of Tin Pan Alley and the Rebirth of the Great American Song* (New York: Riverhead Books), 2015, 117-18.

3. Arthur L. Webb, "The History of Booker T. Washington High School...Part 2," *Tri-State Defender*, March 10, 2004, 1–2.

4. Ellis, William, "Professor W.T. McDaniel," http://memphis-musichalloffame.com/about/

5. Stanley Crouch, "George Coleman Fanmaker," *Village Voice*, May 22, 1984, 67.

6. Dorothy Robinson, interview by Phillip Joyner, 2011.

7. "New Names . . . New Faces," *Pittsburgh Courier, April 5, 1952*, 32.

8. Floyd Newman, interview by Muneer Nasser, September 2011.

9. Willie Thomas, interview by Muneer Nasser, September 18, 2011.

10. Newman, interview.

11. Robinson, interview.

12. Sebastian Danchin, *Blues Boy: The Life and Music of B.B. King* (Jackson: University Press of Mississippi, 1998), 25.

13. B.B. King with David Ritz, *Blues All Around Me: The Autobiography of B.B. King* (New York: HarperCollins, 1996), 175.

14. B.B. King, interview by Muneer Nasser, January 2013.

15. Newman, interview.

16. Ted Panken, "*Today Is the Question: Ted Panken on Music, Politics and the Arts, Interview with George Coleman and Idris Muhammad,*" WKCR, April 5, 1995.

17. Ben Yagoda, *The B Side,* 175.

18. Russ Wilson, "*How Rock Slaughtered Rhythm and Blues,*" *Oakland Tribune,* January 15, 1967, 6.

19. Calvin Newborn, interview by Muneer Nasser, October 2011.

20. Joe Mulherin, "*Newborn Again,*" Memphis, Vol 3 No.4, July 1978, 33.

21. Bruce Mitchell, "Far-out Phineas and the Intellijazzia: It's a Big Jump from Memphis Town," *Esquire,* October 1956.

22. Douglass Henry Daniels, *Lester Leaps In: The Life and Times of Lester Young* (Boston: Beacon Press), 2002.

23. Terry Gibbs and Cary Ginell, *Good Vibes: A Life in Jazz* (Lanham, MD: Scarecrow Press, 2003), 175.

24. Ibid, 23.

25. Leslie Gourse, *Sassy: The Life of Sarah Vaughan* (New York: Da Capo Press), 1994, 83.

26. "Birdland Stars Won't Play Bias Seating Dates; Puts Teeth in Rule," *Chicago Defender*, October 8, 1956, 18.

27. Newborn, interview.

28. Newborn, interview.

29. liner notes for *While My Lady Sleeps* (RCA Victor LPM-1474).

30. "Phineas Newborn Suffers a Nervous Breakdown," *Jet*, November 7, 1957, 57.

31. Julian Euell, interview by Muneer Nasser, November 10, 2011.

32. liner notes for *Soul Junction*, Prestige Records (PRLP7181).

33. Peter Niklas Wilson, *Sonny Rollins: The definitive musical guide*, (Berkley Hills Books, 2001).

34. Leonard Feather, liner notes for *Sonny Rollins Live at the Village Vanguard* (Blue Note 1531).

35. Lou Donaldson, interview by Muneer Nasser, April 18, 2011.

36. Randy Weston, interview by Muneer Nasser, March 2007.

37. Orin Keepnews, liner notes for *Pieces of Eighty-Eight*, Riverside Records, 1959.

38. "Charles Crosby Is In with His Drums," *Cleveland Call and Post*, October 21, 1959, 5A.

39. Jesse H. Walker, "Theatricals," *Amsterdam News,* June 21, 1958, 13.

40. Dizzy Gillespie and Al Fraser, *To Be or Not to Bop,* (University of Minnesota, 2009), 291.

41. Ibid, 292.

42. Ibid, 294.

43. Jamil Nasser, interview by Muneer Nasser, April 2003.

44. Ancestry.com *Florida State Census,* 1867-1945, http://search. ancestry.com/cgi-bin/sse.dll?h=113521&db=FloridaStateCen 1867&indiv=try.

45. Cal Adams, "Local Boy Penned a New Tune That's Catching on Here," *St. Petersburg Times,* December 12, 1956, 50.

46. Amanda R. Howard, *St. Petersburg Times April* 4, 1944, 51.

47. Ibid, 19.

48. *St. Petersburg Times,* December 12, 1943, 19.

49. E.H. McLin, "Local Friends Receive News of Cooper," *St. Petersburg Times,* August 26, 1945, 28.

50. Ibid, 48.

51. "One World Group Gives a Concert," *Evening Independent,* April 6, 1945, 9.

52. "Pinellas Park Tea Slated Today," *St. Petersburg Times,* October 16, 1954.

53. Paul Jeffrey, interview by Muneer Nasser, 2012.

54. Ellsworth Brown, interview by Dartanyan Brown, 2002.

55. Norman Simmons, interview by Muneer Nasser, October 2008.

56. James Harper, "Feeling Life's Beat with Jazzman Idrees Sulieman," *St. Petersburg Times*, September 10, 1984, 38.

57. Amy Elliot, "Still Looking for That Bo' Hog Grind," *Blues Access*, Spring 1998.

58. Donald Dooley, "Hampton's Jumping Jazz Sends 800 Flying Home," *Milwaukee Journal*, February 2, 1959, 16.

59. Jamil Nasser, interview by Phil Schaap, WKCR, March 16, 2001.

60. Schaap, interview.

61. Weston, interview.

62. Harper, "Feeling Life's Beat with Jazzman Idrees Sulieman."

63. Greg Henderson, Idrees Sulieman, *Cadence Magazine*, September 1979, Vol.5 No.9, 6-7.

64. John Handy, interview by Muneer Nasser, November 3, 2011.

65. Nels Nelson, "Sulieman the Magnificent the 'Legendary Trumpeter' Is a Walking History of Music," *Philadelphia Daily News*, June 13, 1990, 40.

66. Peterman, "Idrees Sulieman."

67. Peggy Peterman, "Heyday of Jazz Remembered," *St. Petersburg Times,* May 17, 1978, 38.

68. Nelson, "Sulieman the Magnificent."

69. Nelson, "Sulieman the Magnificent."

70. Ted Panken, "Today Is The Question: Ted Panken on Music, Politics and the Arts, Conversation with Lou Donaldson" for Smithsonian Jazz Oral History Project, June, 20,21, 2012.

71. Craig Basse, "Early Bebop Trumpeter Dies at 78," *St. Petersburg Times,* July 27, 2002.

72. Leslie Gourse, *Straight, No Chaser: The Life and Genius of Thelonious Monk* (Schirmer Trade Books. 1998), 28.

73. Jamil Nasser, interview by Muneer Nasser, April 2003.

74. Webster Young, interview by Muneer Nasser, 1992.

75. Jamila Sulieman, interview by Muneer Nasser, April 2003.

76. John Chilton, *The Song of the Hawk: The Life and Times of Coleman Hawkins* (Ann Arbor: University of Michigan Press, 1990), 286–87.

77. Noal Cohen and Michael Fitzgerald, *Rat Race Blues: The Musical Life of Gigi Gryce* (Berkeley Hills: Berkley Hills 2002), 207.

78. Buster Smith, interview by Muneer Nasser, April 2003.

79. Frank Buchmann-Moller, *You Just Fight for Your Life: The Story of Lester Young* (New York: Praeger), 219.

80. Penny Von Eschen, *Satchmo Blows Up the World: Jazz Ambassadors Play the Cold War* (Cambridge: Harvard University Press, 2004), 7.

81. Ibid, 28.

82. Ibid, 33.

83. Jacques Muyal, liner notes for *Legendary Oscar Dennard*, 1987.

84. Von Eschen, *Satchmo Blows Up the World*, 66.

85. David Stafford, "Satchmo in the Republic of the Congo," 1960 WWOZ Blog, 7/26/2013.

86. Eugene Holley Jr., "Armstrong Akwaba (Welcome)!" *Village Voice Jazz Supplement*, June 12, 2001.

87. Michael Parenti, *Democracy for the Few* (New York: St. Martin's Press, 1977), 163.

88. Jamil Nasser, interview by Muneer Nasser, April 2003.

89. Statement by Adam Markowicz at panel discussion on Oscar Dennard. New York City, April 2003.

90. Von Eschen, *Satchmo Blows Up the World*, 92.

91. Russian-American Jazz Summit featuring Cyril Moshkow and Larry Applebaum," Library of Congress, January 14, 2010, YouTube, http://www.youtube.com/watch?v=xAxJOqR49iw.

92. History of Jazz in Russia, http://www.jazz.ru/eng/

93. "Mitchell and Ruff Duo Upsets Moscow Conservatory Students," *Jet*, July 16, 1959, 60–61.

94. Willie Ruff, *A Call to Assembly* (New Haven: Yale University Press, 1991), 308.

95. Harper, "Feeling Life's Beat with Jazzman Idrees Sulieman."

96. Tim Weiner, *Legacy of Ashes: The History of the CIA* (New York: Doubleday, 2007), 127.

97. Ibid, 283.

98. Tony Brown's Journal, "Malcom X-Karl Evanzz: The Judas Factor," February 23, 2016, https//you.be/NkxZizDfXBO.

99. Department of State, "Report of the Death of an American Citizen," November 16, 1960.

100. Jamil Nasser and Buster Smith, interview by Muneer Nasser, April 2003.

101. John Tynan, "On the Road with Helen Merrill," *DownBeat*, October 10, 1963, 18.

102. Buddy Collette and Steven Isoardi, *jazz generations: a life in american music and society*, (London: Continuum, 2000), 159-163.

103. Gian Mario Maletto, "Virtuosi neri nel jazz internazionale," unidentified Italian newspaper, ca. 1961.

104. Lillian Terry, interview by Muneer Nasser, December 2009.

105. Llewellyn W. Wilson, "Haitian Fortuna Stars in Folies," *Baltimore Afro-American,* June 18, 1946, 5.

106. Monty Alexander, interview by Muneer Nasser, December 2011.

107. Norval Perkins, liner notes for *Naked City Theme,* (Cadet DJLP-733) June 1964.

108. John King, "Jamal shows his Teeth," *Melody Maker,* August 1970.

109. "Ahmad Jamal, "In Pops Concert Wednesday," *The Call and Post,* July 31, 1965, 14B.

110. John King, "Jamal shows his Teeth."

111. Ralph J. Gleason, "Jamal's Avant Garde Stylings Reach Average Listener," *Milwaukee Journal,* October 15, 1965, 54.

112. Frank Gant, interview by Muneer Nasser, December 2006.

113. Don Morrison, "Pray Don't Miss Jamal-He Is 'Up,'" *The Minneapolis Star,* April 26, 1967, 18C.

114. John King, "Jamal shows his teeth."

115. Gant, interview.

116. "U.S. Jazz Musician Reported Arrested," *Washington Post,* June 9, 1967, A2.

117. "Jamal Records Signs with Ampeg Tapes," December 20, 1969, 22.

118. "Sonny Stitt signs with Jamal Records," *New York Amsterdam News*, November 1969, 17.

119. Phone conversation with Ahmad Jamal, October 2011.

120. "Pianist Enters Record Production Business," *New Journal and Globe*, April 18, 1970, 14.

121. *Jet Magazine*, April 9, 1970.

122. Leslie Gourse, *Straight, No Chaser*, 284.

123. Robin D.G. Kelley, *Thelonious Monk: The Life and Times of an American Original*, (New York: Free Press, 2009), 434.

124. Paul Jeffrey, interview by Muneer Nasser, February 1, 2012.

125. Randy Weston and Willard Jenkins, *African Rhythms: The Autobiography of Randy Weston* (Durham: Duke University Press, 2010), 184.

126. Owen McNally, "Old and New Jazz Groups Play Here," *Hartford Courant*, April 21, 1975, 22.

127. Ivey Avery, "Ahmad Jamal," *Utimme Umana La Voz Oculta*, November 1973.

128. Bob Matthews, "...All That Jazz," *Baltimore African-American*, April 24, 1976, 17.

129. Sanford Josephson, "Jazz Veteran Al Haig Is Still Bopping," *Eastside Courier*, March 24, 1977, 12.

130. Leonard Feather, "Shepherd Takes Road to Memphis," *Los Angeles Times*, February 10, 1980, M5.

131. John Wilson, "Jazz: Cybill Shepherd," *New York Times*, December 21, 1979, 10.

132. Bill Rhoden, "Louis Hayes's new quartet is playing the Bandstand," *Baltimore Sun*, March 21, 1979, B6.

133. Owen McNally, "Strozier Sax Lights Night," *The Hartford Courant*, April 18, 1979, 58.

134. Owen McNally, "Trumpets Reign at (and After) Monday's Rained-On Concerts," *The Hartford Courant*, August 1, 1991, 8.

135. John S. Wilson, "Jazz 4: Eddie Vinson," August 8, 1981, 28.

136. Owen McNally, "Ashby on Tenor Sax: Among the Very Best in Big Band Tradition," *The Hartford Courant*, August 1, 1984, 8.

137. Howard Mandel, "Freddie Hubbard New Direction, Fresh Perspective," *DownBeat*, June 15, 1978, 15.

138. Ted Panken, "Today is the Question," interview with Freddie Hubbard, *DownBeat*, 2001.

139. Quincy Troupe, *Miles* (New York: Simon and Schuster, 1989), 262.

140. Sid Lazard, liner notes for *Fantastic* Frank Strozier-plus (VeeJay records), December 9, 1959.

141. Angela Parker, "Ben Branch and Sax Stirs Civil Rights Movement." *Chicago Tribune*, September 23, 1971, S1.

142. Wanda Rushing, *Memphis and the Paradox of Place: Globalization in the Amercan South,* (North Carolina Press, 2010), 230.

143. Walter Dawson, "Beale Street: Memphis Razes Blues Landmark," *Rolling Stone Magazine*, Issue 140, August 1973, 21.

144. Fred J. Hay, *"Goin' Back to Memphis: Conversations with the Blues,"* (University of Georgia Press,2005), 25 of intro.

145. Michael Finger, "A Look Back at the Early Days of the Memphis in May Barbeque Cooking Contest," www.memphismagazine.com, 12/28/10.

146. Jonathan Devin, "Memphis in May,": Where it's been and how it's doing," Vol.125, no.90, May 10,2010.

147. Robert Palmer, "Memphis Its Old Jazzy Self for 2 Days," *New York Times*, May 26, 1982. C25.

148. Irvin Salky, interview by Muneer Nasser, October 2011.

149. Michael Arnold, "Crowd is Assurance Orpheum will Shine," *Memphis Commercial Appeal*, December 1978, 15.

150. Robert Palmer, "Beale Street History Repeats Itself for a Weekend," *Sarasota Herald-Tribune,* June 7, 1978, 28.

151. Rhashidah E. McNeil, "Self Portraits: The last day," June 5, 1989.

152. Ernie Santosuosso, "Three African Queens," *Boston Globe*, July 10, 1981, 1.

153. Randy Weston, interview by Muneer Nasser, March 2007.

154. Deborah Kapchan, *Traveling Spirit Masters: Moroccan Ganawa Trance Music and Music in the Global* (Wesleyan University Press, 2005), 274.

155. Doug Ramsey, "Seeing Red," *Texas Monthly*, March 1977, 22.

156. Lou Donaldson, interview by Muneer Nasser, April 18, 2011.

157. Hollie I. West, "Jazz Duo at Blues Alley," *Washington Post*, May 25, 1977, B6.

158. Robert Palmer, "Once and Future Wizard," *New York Times*, April 21, 1978, 26.

159. Booth, "Fascinating Changes," 21.

160. Ernie Santosuosso, "There's More to Memphis Then Elvis and Dinah Shore; Memphis Piano Summit," *Boston Globe*, October 12, 1981, 1.

161. James Reese, "Phineas, "Le Sphinx de Memphis," *Jazz Hot*, April 1983, 30–31.

162. Jamil Nasser, interview by Muneer Nasser, April 2003.

163. John S. Wilson, "Critics Choice," *New York Times*, May 27, 1984.

164. Owen McNally, "Donaldson Still Sings Like Bird," *The Hartford Courant*, April 27, 1982, B12.

165. Carol A. Miller, *South African Music: A Century of Traditions in Transformation* (Santa Barbara, 2004), 40.

166. "Building the Cultural Boycott," *Southern Africa,* Jan-Feb 1983, 3-6.

167. Howard "Duke" Anderson, *Stream of Consciousness*, October 20, 1992.

168. Sue Steward, "Monty Alexander's Ivory and Steel: a musical celebration of the west indies," concert program.

169. Monty Alexander, interview by Muneer Nasser, 2011.

170. George Coleman Sr., interview by Muneer Nasser, 2011.

171. Richard M. Sudhalter, "Tenor Reigned Supreme," *New York Post,* January 16, 1979, 59.

172. Coleman Sr., interview.

173. Ted Panken, "Today Is the Question: Ted Panken on Music, Politics and the Arts, interview with George Coleman and Idris Muhammad," WKCR, April 5, 1995.

174. Herb Boyd, "Flock of Bird lovers roost at Pier 17," *Amsterdam News,* June 27, 1992, 28.

175. Peter Watrous, "Jazz and Pop Review," *New York Times,* January 9, 1992.

176. Alfred Appel, *Jazz Modernism: From Ellington and Armstrong to Matisse and Joyce,* (Yale University Press, 2004), 261.

177. Jimmy Owens, interview by Muneer Nasser, June 2010

178. Herb F. Storfer, "A Few Words about the Jazz Musicians Emergency Fund."

179. Owens, interview.

180. "Hospital Reaches Out to Jazz Musicians in Need," *New York Times*, April 6, 1994.

181. George Kanzler, "Thornton triumphant as master jazz storyteller," *The Star Ledger*, December 3, 1998, 63.

182. Teri Thornton, interview by Fred Jung, *All About Jazz /Jazz Magazine and Resource*. http;//www.allaboutjazz.com/iviews/TThornton.htm.

183. Atiba Taylor, interview by Muneer Nasser, February 11, 2011.

184. Conversation with Cheyney Thomas, June 2010.

185. George Coleman Jr., interview by Muneer Nasser, March 21, 2010.

186. William A. Brower, Arts & Entertainment, *The Washington Informer*, May 5-11, 1983, 19.

187. Paul Cantrell, "Jazzocide," *New Times*, November 13, 1984, 116-117.

188. Ibid, 116-117.

189. Jim Mason, "Concert by Sanders Inspiring," *Richmond News Leader*, May 2, 1980, 38.

190. Dr. Martin Luther King Jr., quote from address at the 1964 Berlin Jazz Festival.

191. Papa Jo Jones, interview by Muneer Nasser, June 1984.

192. Peter Watrous, "The Elusive Lucky Thompson," *Village Voice*, June 26, 1984, 74.

193. Ibid, 191.

194. Dan Morganstern, "Lucky Thompson says Later for the Music Business," *DownBeat*, January 13, 1966, 11.

195. Max Jones, *Talking Jazz: Profiles, Interviews, and other Riffs on Jazz Musicians*, (Macmillan Press, 1987), 75.

196. Norma Jean Darden, "Hazel Scott: Up Tempo," *Essence Magazine*, November 1978, 76.

197. Ibid, 77.

198. "Racial Prejudice in Jazz," *DownBeat*, March 29, 1962, 24-25.

199. Umar Nasser, interview by Muneer Nasser, 2012.

200. Zaid Nasser, interview by Muneer Nasser, September 17, 2017.

Index

Index

Index

Index

Index

Index

Index

Index

207-208; on Azzedin joining
Jamal, 128-129; portrait series,
151; 191; Spoleto, 150; Weston on
Jamil, 151; with Boston Pops, 150
whiskey, 45
White Rose Café, 7
white woman, 30-31
White, Maurice, 1,141
Whitfield, Lynn, 205
Wilen, Barney, 73
Willhite, Lee, 189
Williams, Florence C., 47
Williams, Jackie, 209
Williams, James, 162
Williams, Joe, 20, 22
Williams, John, 150
Williams, Mary Lou, 56
Williams, Nate D., 8, 146
Williams, Richard "Notes," ix
Williams, Tommy, 115
Willisau Festival, 136
Wilson, Gerald, 206
Wilson, Nancy, 119
Wilson, Shadow, 18
Wilson, Willie "Silly," 12
Winding, Kai, 115
"Woke up this Morning," 15, 174
Wonder, Stevie, 159, 175

Woodard, Nathan, 8, 147
Wooding, Sam, 67
Woods, Chris, 141
Woodyard, Sam, 30
Workman, Reggie, 128
Wotton, Red, 50
Wricks, John, (maternal grandfather), 2
Wricks, Marianna, (maternal
grandmother), 2
Wyands, Richard, 113, 209

X

X, Malcolm, Jamil meets Malcolm X,
43-44, 170

Y

Yacub's history, 43
Young Jeezy, 130
Young, Evelyn, 13
Young, Lester, 17, 22, checked
by, 29; George on Lester, 23;
56; ilness and death of, 59; last
recording of, 59; 169, 183
Young, Webster, 57

Z

Zain El Abidin Cemetery, 71
Zurich, 65

Made in the USA
Middletown, DE
18 June 2020

96685244R00156